Measures and Metrics in Corporate Security

Second Edition

T0348734

Measures and Metrics in Corporate Security

Second Edition

George K. Campbell

ELSEVIER

AMSTERDAM • BOSTON • HEIDELBERG • LONDON
NEW YORK • OXFORD • PARIS • SAN DIEGO
SAN FRANCISCO • SINGAPORE • SYDNEY • TOKYO

Security
Executive Council

Elsevier
225 Wyman Street, Waltham, MA, 02451, USA
The Boulevard, Langford Lane, Kidlington, Oxford, OX5 1GB, UK

Originally published by the Security Executive Council in 2006.

Notices
Knowledge and best practice in this field are constantly changing. As new research and experience broaden our understanding, changes in research methods or professional practices, or medical treatment may become necessary.

Practitioners and researchers must always rely on their own experience and knowledge in evaluating and using any information or methods, compounds, or experiments described herein. In using such information or methods they should be mindful of their own safety and the safety of others, including parties for whom they have a professional responsibility.

To the fullest extent of the law, neither the Publisher nor the authors, contributors, or editors, assume any liability for any injury and/or damage to persons or property as a matter of products liability, negligence or otherwise, or from any use or operation of any methods, products, instructions, or ideas contained in the material herein.

Library of Congress Cataloging-in-Publication Data
Campbell, George, 1942-
   Measures and metrics in corporate security / George K. Campbell. -- Second edition.
      pages cm
   "Originally published by the Security Executive Council in 2006."
   Includes bibliographical references and index.
   ISBN 978-0-12-800688-7 (alk. paper)
1.   Corporations--Security measures. 2.   Business enterprises--Security measures. 3.   Security systems--Management. I. Title.
   HD61.5.C363 2014
   658.4'7--dc23   2014005929
Printed and bound by CPI Group (UK) Ltd, Croydon, CR0 4YY

British Library Cataloguing-in-Publication Data
A catalogue record for this book is available from the British Library

ISBN: 978-0-12-800688-7

This book has been manufactured using Print On Demand technology. Each copy is produced to order and is limited to black ink. The online version of this book will show color figures where appropriate.

Working together
to grow libraries in
developing countries

www.elsevier.com • www.bookaid.org

Contents

Acknowledgments

I owe a debt of gratitude to Bob Hayes, Kathleen Kotwica (K2), Francis D'Addario, and Liz Lancaster at the Security Executive Council for supporting my work in this space. And special thanks to my very special team at Fidelity Investments Corporate Security, who gave more than just meaning and results to metrics.

Since this is a second edition, this book has been circulating for several years among an ever-wider readership and within a variety of corporate security environments. Of significance for me, the first edition laid a foundation for far more in-depth testing, affirmation, and modification of ideas about measuring security programs and communicating our value. That learning will be found in my next book on security metrics, which takes a much deeper dive into building a program and providing examples.

The concept for this book was developed by:

Robert Hayes
Managing Director
Security Executive Council

This book was edited by:

Kathleen Kotwica, PhD
Executive Vice President and Chief Knowledge Strategist
Security Executive Council

About the Author

George Campbell served until 2002 as the chief security officer at Fidelity Investments, the largest mutual fund company in the United States with more than $2 trillion in customer assets and 32,500 employees. Under Campbell's leadership, the global corporate security organization delivered a wide range of proprietary services including information security, disaster recovery planning and crisis management, criminal investigations, fraud prevention, and more. Since leaving Fidelity, Campbell has served as a content expert for the Security Executive Council, of which he is a founding Emeritus Faculty member.

Prior to working at Fidelity Investments, Campbell owned a security and consulting firm, which specialized in risk assessment and security program management. He has also been group vice president at a system engineering firm that supported government security programs at high-threat sites around the world. Early on in his career, Campbell worked in the criminal justice system, and served in various line and senior management positions within federal, state, and local government agencies.

Campbell received his bachelor's degree in police administration from American University in Washington, DC. He served on the Board of Directors of the International Security Management Association (ISMA), and as ISMA's president in 2003. Campbell is also a long-time member of ASIS International. He is a former member of the National Council on Crime Prevention, the High Technology Crime Investigation Association, and the Association of Certified Fraud Examiners, and is an alumnus of the US State Department's Overseas Security Advisory Council.

Digital Assets

Thank you for selecting *Measures and Metrics in Corporate Security*, second edition. To complement the learning experience, we have provided a number of customizable PowerPoint Slide presentations with sample metrics from *Measures and Metrics in Corporate Security*.

These presentations provide a template for you to use to communicate as managers and advisors on risk. They have been designed to easily plug in your own program data, terms, company name, company logo, etc. They have also been field tested by experts and were found to resonate with senior management. The examples in each slideshow have been genericized from real company presentations.

Key Features
- Provide recommendations for the application of each presentation.
- Charts are customizable.
- Include Security Executive Council faculty coaching notes on how to use each metric effectively.

These online materials are available at: http://booksite.elsevier.com/9780128006887.

Preface

There are three kinds of lies:
Lies, damn lies, and statistics

Benjamin Disraeli

This book is a starting point for ideas and notes on what works and what may not work in the development and application of measures and metrics in security.

If the concept of a shared, collaborative volume works, this book will look very different and be significantly improved in future editions. Ideally, it will fall into the hands of nonsecurity professionals who have creativity, skills, and techniques transferable to the security space and need, including students exploring security administration, interested corporate governance colleagues, risk managers, corporate counsels, security consultants, trade associations, and others with an increasingly vested interest in the business of corporate protection. It would be particularly valuable if we could obtain feedback from business executives on what measures and metrics they need to see from their security managers. We hope it will be due to the success of our readers in better informing their management team about risk management that will provide such feedback.

As for me, I cannot even balance a checkbook and when I have had the risk-*mis*managed opportunity to control one, I typically run it out for several months and then terminate it with extreme prejudice. I can then start anew with something close to historical accommodation with the bank's balance for a month or two. So, having me author a primer on security metrics likely brings literary fraud to new heights.

However, over the years, I have been blessed with incredibly bright colleagues and coworkers and a set of corporate expectations that accentuate excellence and eliminate the hiding places known as cost centers. Security operations are value centers when their leaders recognize their place in the scheme of corporate integrity, proactive risk management, and profitability contribution. But the measures and metrics that might support the performance objectives of these business-centered security executives are being brought into a limited intellectual debate. While the full-service security organization is a franchise player in the focus on the corporate governance infrastructure, it does not typically enjoy a place at the table in the ongoing discussion of internal controls and governance.

The fact that there is no accepted model for corporate security organizations delays the debate and the thoughtful consideration of how various security programs contribute to a measurable, integrated picture of enterprise protection. This volume alone will not change the picture, but it will hopefully aid progressive security executives (and others) as they engage and think about security's value equation.

George Campbell

Introduction

Over the past several years, the more I have worked with some really good security organizations to assess and develop their metrics programs, the more I am convinced that metrics is not about the numbers, it is about measuring performance of people, process, and performance. Do not get me wrong, we need to build and maintain lists of numbers, but this is just the beginning of the work. Like a smart colleague of mine says, "It's just counting nails." What do these numbers mean? What story do they tell, what action is required and by whom?

Much of what follows in this book is focused on examples of security management challenges and opportunities and the role and contribution I see for measurements and metrics. But I think it is important to level set where you stand in terms of your program's status whether you are reading this as a security executive with a solid metrics program, some one desiring to reinvent or build a body of security metrics or perhaps as a student of the discipline. In working with scores of corporate security organizations over the past decade, I have found that there are about a dozen questions about a security organization's metrics program that effectively serve to focus the manager on developmental priorities. It is a logical beginning to this book and aids in consideration of the potential value of the examples that are discussed throughout.

Metrics program assessment

> What is the business case for your security organization and how do you want it measured? What are the quantifiable measurements that ought to apply to management's assessment of value? How would you grade your measurements and metrics?

The following metrics self-assessment tool walks the security manager through a number of questions about how they would rank their program's maturity. Take an honest look at each of the descriptions and see how you would assess your current security metrics program. If you think carefully about the questions and your assessment compared to the alternatives, I think you will find a road map for targeted improvements.

You can work this assessment on your own if you are a sole practitioner. But if you have a team of managers leading various programs and functions, it would be advisable to develop this as a team exercise. It will get everyone (hopefully) on the same page and likely identify a host of strengths, weaknesses, opportunities, and threats (SWOT). This self-assessment is a precursor to the metrics construction process that takes the reader through six steps in building a program. Use it to leverage your strengths and opportunities and note where each of the steps offers an approach to mitigating your weaknesses and threats.

Review and fill in the attached self-assessment questionnaire. Select the statement that best suits your situation and designate the current level of accomplishment for your selection. For example, if you selected "1.2 Management is beginning to seek performance measures and metrics from security," a Level 1 would indicate you are at the earliest stage of response to this need. If none fit the bill, insert your own selection as noted.

Key Metrics Program Indicators	Maturity Level		
1. Organizational Context	Level 1	Level 2	Level 3
1.1 Metrics are an accepted element within selected business operations but have not been requested from security			
1.2 Management is beginning to seek performance measures and metrics from security			
1.3 Performance measures and metrics are a required element of program management			
(Insert your own performance indicator if not listed or adaptable above)			
2. Current Status of Metrics Within the Security Department	Level 1	Level 2	Level 3
2.1 Recognized need and trying to understand best first steps			
2.2 Established objective but just in very early stages of development			
2.3 We have a variety of data and now are moving to identify best approach for desired results			
2.4 We have several focused metrics outputs for targeted constituents but now want to elevate the content and management (or board) targeting			
2.5 We have a well-established program with quality reporting and now desire to develop a more directed and influential set of measures and metrics			
(Insert your own performance indicator if not listed or adaptable above)			
3. Data Availability	Level 1	Level 2	Level 3
3.1 We do not currently have a centralized incident reporting system			
3.2 We have a limited incident reporting database that is distributed among multiple security-related functions			
3.3 We have an enterprise-wide incident reporting and case management system that enables reporting of desired metrics			

Key Metrics Program Indicators	Maturity Level		
(Insert your own performance indicator if not listed or adaptable above)			
4. Data Reliability	Level 1	Level 2	Level 3
4.1 Our incident and performance-related data do not currently have consistent standards of review and reliability			
4.2 Although our incident and performance-related data are distributed among multiple organizational units, there are consistent standards of review and reliability for reporting up			
4.3 We have an enterprise-wide incident and performance-related data repository with consistent standards of review and reliability			
(Insert your own performance indicator if not listed or adaptable above)			
5. Analytical Scope and Discipline	Level 1	Level 2	Level 3
5.1 Current processing of incident and performance data is primarily limited to maintaining counts of various data elements for trend analysis and reporting			
5.2 A limited number of security programs are thoroughly analyzed for qualitative and quantitative findings and targeted reporting			
5.3 Selected security programs have established performance measurement criteria and are consistently tracked and subjected to in-depth analysis			
5.4 All security programs are subjected to ongoing qualitative and quantitative measurement with metrics outputs available for management reporting			
(Insert your own performance indicator if not listed or adaptable above)			
6. Analytical Benefits	Level 1	Level 2	Level 3
6.1 While it is an objective, we do not currently provide a measurable level of analysis to our incident and program performance data			
6.2 We see measurable results when we provide analyses of business unit risk exposure and security advice to business units			
6.3 Our analyses provide evidence of compliance with applicable regulations			
6.4 Our analyses provide evidence of business unit compliance with policies related to internal controls and security			

Continued

—cont'd

Key Metrics Program Indicators	Maturity Level		
6.5 Our analyses of security program performance has enabled demonstrably improved management understanding of the value of security investments			
6.6 Our ongoing analyses of risk assessment and security program performance data are a required deliverable to senior management (and the board)			
(Insert your own performance indicator if not listed or adaptable above)			
7. Reporting	Level 1	Level 2	Level 3
7.1 Reporting is primarily for internal security department program performance tracking			
7.2 There are multiple security functions with no consolidated metrics reporting			
7.3 Formal reporting of program performance data is limited to a select few key indicators required by management			
7.4 We provide a variety of standardized and tailored metrics reports to management on an established schedule			
(Insert your own performance indicator if not listed or adaptable above)			
8. Directional Performance– Standards and Guidelines	Level 1	Level 2	Level 3
8.1 We have not found a set of security-related standards or guidelines that may be useful as measurement benchmarks			
8.2 We currently do no employ an established body of industry or locally developed performance standards or guidelines that may be used as benchmark targets for metrics			
8.3 We have adopted a selected set of measurable performance standards or guidelines developed by others that are tracked and reported to management			
8.4 We have both adopted externally produced performance standards and developed others appropriate to our unique business management requirements			

Key Metrics Program Indicators	Maturity Level		
(Insert your own performance indicator if not listed or adaptable above)			
9. Actionability	Level 1	Level 2	Level 3
9.1 Our metrics are limited to occasional reports that are primarily designed to inform on status of selected trends over time			
9.2 We are in the process of developing a body of metrics that may be used to measure the value and effectiveness of security programs			
9.3 Our metrics are primarily analyzed and delivered to affirm positive business unit action or advise and direct corrective actions			
(Insert your own performance indicator if not listed or adaptable above)			
10. Resources and Tools	Level 1	Level 2	Level 3
10.1 Resource constraints currently limit our ability to maintain an effective security metrics program			
10.2 Each security manager is required to maintain basic performance metrics for each of their assigned programs			
10.3 We devote adequate staff time and employ a robust set of applications to maintain and deliver a variety of metrics reports to management			
10.4 Our company has developed dashboard models that we are adapting to suit our security metrics reporting requirements			
(Insert your own performance indicator if not listed or adaptable above)			
11. Data Sensitivity and Protection	Level 1	Level 2	Level 3
11.1 There are safeguards that protect the confidentiality of metrics data that could reveal potentially risky information to unauthorized individuals			
(Insert your own performance indicator if not listed or adaptable above)			
12. Summary Assessment–Measuring Security's Value to the Enterprise	Level 1	Level 2	Level 3
12.1 We are actively seeking a body of metrics capable of demonstrating measurable value to the enterprise			
12.2 We have a body of metrics accepted by management as demonstrating measurable value to the enterprise			

Continued

—cont'd

Key Metrics Program Indicators	Maturity Level
(Insert your own performance indicator if not listed or adaptable above)	
Organization: Evaluator: Date:	

Using this assessment

If you are just beginning this hunt for your few meaningful metrics, you need to carefully consider the implications of your choices. For example, consider your selection of these options:

3.1 We do not currently have a centralized incident reporting system;

4.1 Our incident and performance-related data do not currently have consistent standards of review and reliability; and

5.1 Current processing of incident and performance data is primarily limited to maintaining counts of various data elements for trend analysis and reporting.

The absence of a centralized reporting system is not a show-stopper but the lack of an effective incident reporting system is. In the former, you have the data spread among various entities but it will be more difficult to bring it into a form that enables solid analysis. In the latter, you likely cannot rely on the data it is going to be difficult to even gather; thus the likely selection of 4.1. When you have the data and you are confident of its accuracy, remember that after you put it in a form that essentially enables counting, that is only the beginning. Counts are okay for trending but do not provide direction for alternative action; they merely serve up the fuel for your analysis and decisions.

> Reliability is the heart of a metrics program so that is your first priority in the building process.

Every one of these assessment items has its own implications for your next steps. If you are alone in interpreting your results or the team needs some thoughtful advice, think about the short story above and find a mentor who can help you sort the options and be a supporter in the construction process. If you are in great shape, check out the examples and hopefully find a number of ideas for adding and improving your security metrics portfolio.

Building your program

If you have come away from the assessment with a conclusion that you have a mature, well functioning metrics program that is delivering measurable results to you as a manager and to your customers, I suggest you use the table of contents to

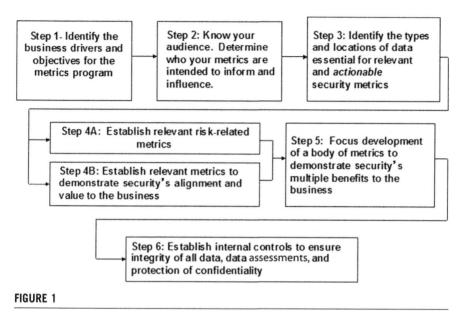

FIGURE 1

Construction process for implementing a security measures and metrics program.

cherry pick topics that I hope will deliver an actionable idea or two. If the assessment helped you focus on some gaps or shortcomings or if you are engaged in a bottoms-up reinvention, perhaps a review of the following (Figure 1) will find an approach to set your program in the right direction.

Step 1: Identify the business drivers and objectives for the security metrics program

Where can metrics deliver the greatest benefits for your company and the security mission?

- Is to make a positive impact on company policy and culture?
- Or should it be to measurably impact risk exposure?
- How about to demonstrate security's alignment with business goals and bringing value to the bottom line?
- How about all of these and more?

Look at the key words in Figure 2: risk, measure, value, policy, influence, impact, change, compliance, alignment, and strategy. These are the high profile targets of your metrics.

Be clear on your priorities and objectives as you begin to develop your program. Talk to your boss and probe what management would value and how they would use actionable metrics from your organization. Learn who of your colleagues is measuring and reporting with quality and relevance. I will give you a tip that your information security partner has volumes of established metrics you can use as a model.

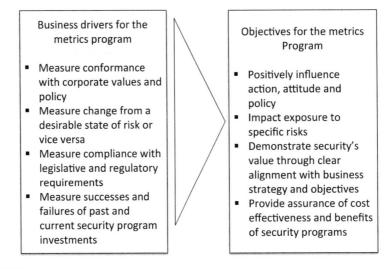

FIGURE 2

Step 1: Identify the business drivers and objectives for the metrics program.

Do not take this step lightly. Create a formal process for identifying what management wants and needs. Think about the knowledge resident in your programs that offer quality guidance to business strategy and an improved state of risk management. There is a clear correlation between how well you identify these needs and how successful your program will be.

Step 2: Determine whom your metrics are intended to inform and influence

You are well aware of what will happen if your company fails to connect with the needs of its customers. I cannot overemphasize the importance of understanding the diversity of perceptions about risk and how each of your constituents view your role in its management. Metrics are central to our ability to influence and engage our customers in their role in corporate security and brand protection. They enable a coherent set of messages focused on a targeted audience.

Each of these audiences (see Figure 3) has a unique agenda and set of needs, a "hot button," if you will. Some need to see the broader view with a clear assessment of alternatives. Others require the 10 min laser approach to the problem and best solution. You must know your customer and what motivates them to action. Your message has to be tailored to influence, to enable them to see why your message deserves their acceptance and buy-in.

Metrics should be presented as enabling tools rather than criticisms whenever possible. Positive action is more likely if the audience feels he or she is being given an opportunity rather than a sharp stick in the eye. You want partnership in results more than a notch on the gun.

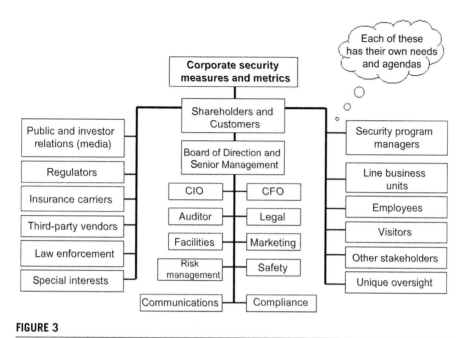

FIGURE 3

Step 2: Know your audience. Determine whom your metrics are intended to inform and influence. (Note: CIO is chief information officer, CFO is chief financial officer.)

Step 3: Identify the types and locations of data essential for *actionable* security metrics

I have no time for the security manager that tells me there are no data to support a metrics program! Now, I will take that back if you do not log calls, take reports on incidents and are not accountable for reporting on how you have spent your budget; in which case the remainder of this presentation has no connection to your security program. You have a staggering amount of data in the files associated with your service portfolio. You have invested financial, personnel, and technology resources into understanding, preventing, and responding to the risks on your watch and the services you provide to your customers (Figure 4).

Take a look at the business drivers and objectives you outlined in step 1, and then consider the types of data you might need in order to create meaningful metrics that help meet those objectives. Think about the needs and hot buttons of your many constituents seen in step 2.

- How have your programs resulted in an improved state of risk management?
- What was learned that should modify business process and thereby eliminate future risk?
- How can your unique knowledge and perspective more directly enable alignment of security programs to the business strategy and needs of your internal customers?

Actionable metrics require analysis, draw conclusions, and tell a story. The results they demonstrate provide direction for decisions, affirm actions taken, or provide

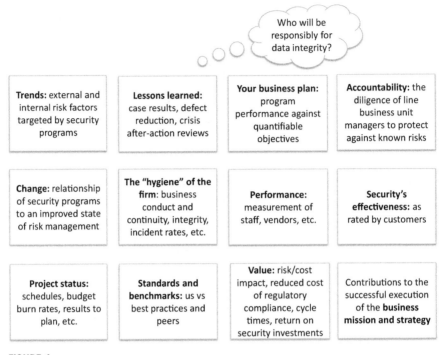

FIGURE 4

Step 3: Identify the types and locations of data essential for relevant and *actionable* security metrics.

clarity for next steps. Nonactionable metrics simply count things and have little value for influencing or finding causes of risk.

This file cabinet represents the various categories of metrics with an emphasis on making them actionable. Develop the contents of each drawer based on your constituents' needs as well as the need to maintain a library of measures consistent with the security organization's needs.

Putting the data to work

So, now I am seeing a trend, a timeline on workplace violence. How do I get to the *meaningful, actionable* metrics? You employ the same process you would follow to build a solution to the problem: what are the root causes, what specific steps or countermeasures should we employ to eliminate these vulnerabilities, and what performance measures would I apply to tell me my proposed solutions were effective? This landscape looks something like Figure 5.

Step 4: Establish relevant risk-related metrics

Relevant metrics clearly link to something you want to accomplish that has a direct benefit to the business. We can approach this step in a couple of ways: (1) establishing

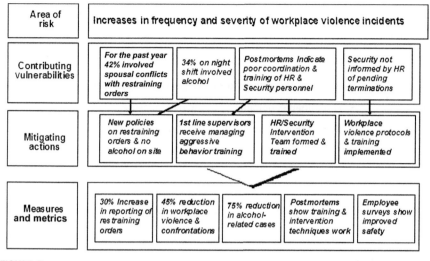

FIGURE 5

Moving from an incident trend to metrics.

metrics that demonstrate our role in enterprise risk management and (2) establishing metrics that demonstrate our alignment with business strategy and objectives.

Risk-related metrics will allow you to determine and to demonstrate to management how security programs and services are impacting the business' risk. To develop these:

1. Prioritize the risks confronting your enterprise. What is the appetite for risk? Which are most important to the business, and which have the greatest potential consequences?
2. Determine which risks security has full or partial responsibility for managing (remember that security is a shared, delegated accountability in several key areas).
3. Inventory the products and services you have in place to address these risks.
4. Identify the results management wants to see from its investment in these products or services; how these products and services are impacting risk management (positively or negatively); and whether they are doing the job reliably and cost effectively.

Your focus on risk also provides an opportunity to demonstrate security's alignment with the business and our value contributions. Can you envision a metric that demonstrates the results of the steps you are taking to reduce or manage program costs while maintaining or improving the state of security in your company?

As you establish your metrics, focus on developing those that could serve the dual purposes of assessing risk and demonstrating value. Highlight metrics that show such benefits as increased protection and decreased cost, enhanced customer satisfaction or confidence due to security measures, increased recovery of losses, reduced risk to revenue-generating activities, reduced insurance costs, reduced risk of attack, and reduced notable audit findings attributable to security defects.

Figure 6 is a summary example.

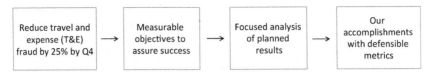

- Based on security **performance goals** and **objectives**
- **Quantifiable,** obtainable, feasible to measure
- **Repeatable,** provide relevant **performance trends** over time
- Useful in **tracking performance** and directing resources

FIGURE 6

Metrics are designed to facilitate decision making and accountability. Adapted from Hash & Grance, National Institute of Standards & Technology.

Step 5: Focus your metrics on demonstrating security's multiple benefits to the business

Our metrics need to be focused on assuring measurable benefits to the business—some are indicators of enhanced levels of protection while others indicate positive reductions in cost and risk exposure.

- They drive setting standards and facilitate the critical assessment of program performance.
- They set expectations for owners and operators of risky business processes.
- They set objectives that result in improved response, faster recovery, and lower cost of business operations.
- They facilitate measurement of qualitative and quantitative results that may serve to support a variety of business objectives while providing measurable direction to program implementation.
- They enable measurement of consequences of failed response and the benefits of above standards performance.
- They force consideration of alternative approaches thereby enabling cost avoidance and cost efficiency.
- They facilitate teamwork and management direction by setting visibly measurable objectives and program performance plans.

Look this list over (Figure 7) and see where your programs may contain additive or deductive benefits you can track and report to management.

Step 6: Establish internal controls to ensure integrity of all data, data assessments, and protection of confidentiality

There is an old saying that there are three types of lies: "lies, damn lies, and statistics." I will not dwell on the obvious downside of lies or damn lies in our job, but

Additive benefits	**Deductive benefits**
• Increased level of protection with improved controls and less cost	• Reduced risk to revenue generating activities
• Increased engagement of employees in securing corporate assets	• Reduced cost of security related incidents
• Enhanced ability to satisfy customers with improved methods of protection	• Reduced cost of insurance
• Increased market penetration attributable to security measures	• Reduced notable audit findings attributable to security defects
. Increased recovery time to critical process interruption	• Decreased risk exposure from cost reducing outsourced activities
• Increased integrity to revenue generating activities	• Reduced risk to customers in sensitive transactions & relationship management
• Increased recovery of losses	• Reduced risk of attack through more measurably effective protective measures
• Increased confidence in effectiveness and need for security controls	• Reductions in employee interaction with time consuming security measures

FIGURE 7

Step 5: Focus development of a body of metrics to demonstrate security's multiple benefits to the business.

I will underscore the importance of accuracy and integrity in your use of data and statistics (see Figure 8).

Assurance of accountability

You do not need a dedicated staff or individual to maintain a quality metrics program. If your scope includes the full range of security services or if you are a sole practitioner overseeing the physical security program, specific individuals need to be held accountable for maintaining the administrative integrity related to data to be maintained for metrics and other elements of program management. If you rely heavily on vendors to provide the day-to-day security service delivery, do not fail to incorporate contractual standards on reporting and data administration.

Assurance of data integrity

Consider these two key objectives for our security measures and metrics: (1) positively influence action, attitude, and policy and (2), materially impact exposure to specific risks. The visibility of these objectives imposes the highest standards of data integrity. The ability to craft strategy and tactics that effectively target specific risks relies upon reliable data processed by competent, focused analysis. But imagine the potential consequences of drawing conclusions and formulating recommendations to management on inaccurate, unreliable data overseen by flawed, poorly supervised sources!

Data management and analysis

You can maintain a solid metrics program with standard desktop applications like Excel and PowerPoint. But scalable, commercially available incident reporting

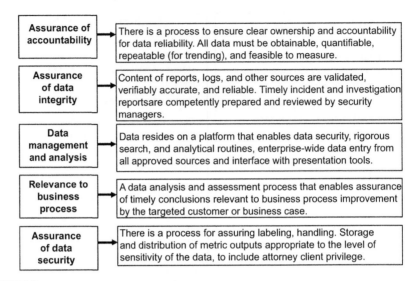

FIGURE 8

Step 6: Establish internal controls to ensure integrity of all data, data assessments, and protection of confidentiality.

software is highly recommended to provide a more tailored and robust infrastructure for standardized reporting, facilitate customized administrative routines and enable quantitative analysis and trending.

Relevance to business process

There are two perspectives with security metrics in my view. One involves the essential maintenance of data to support security program planning, management, and performance assessment. The other analyzes a variety of risk and program-specific data and draws conclusions of *measurable* relevance to business risk management. We seek to structure measures and metrics that inform (increase awareness) and assess the effectiveness of internal controls. Remember, we seek to influence policy and enable the business to more securely engage in business activities that might otherwise be too risky.

> Metrics are the fuel of a corporate security communication strategy. The accuracy and reliability of your data and the conclusions you draw from them, are directly tied to the reliability—the trust—of the security program and its leadership.

Assurance of data security

A measurably effective metrics program will be storing and generating a variety of outputs containing highly sensitive information. Reporting on risk is a risky business, it may reflect on the reputation of the business. Think about a presentation to top management or the board on investigative findings related to employee misconduct or the need to address significant vulnerabilities in the protection of customer information. This is potential stuff for the upper right hand corner of the

Wall Street Journal.[1] As the need for such metrics is identified, you may want to discuss special protection of the files and outputs with general counsel. They may want to apply attorney client privilege for any material that may be generated with regard to reports on matters of high sensitivity. A classification scheme consistent with information protection policy should be applied and, if for some strange reason there is no such policy at your company, you are encouraged to seek guidance on confidentiality labeling, distribution and secure storage. Remember, the data we cull from our logs, incident reports, storage media and other sources we maintain are discoverable in litigation for negligent security or other legal matters.

This last step is primarily about quality assurance and housekeeping. Obviously, there are a lot of devils in the details but these six steps should serve to provide a solid foundation for a security metrics program and, along with the self-assessment, a quality check for what you have in place now. But, if you are going to put this solid program with attentive management to work, it still comes down to that few slides that you present to your audience of one or many. So, I will close with a simple process to use as a guide in this delivery of your results.

A few closing thoughts

If you are not measuring, you are not managing. Measures and metrics are all about directly aiding the consideration of options, processes associated with making effective, defensible decisions and, as a significant benefit for embedded protection supporting an accountability model within our constituent business processes. Metrics reflect quantifiable progress toward goals and they facilitate trending for performance navigation and tracking.

A qualitative security measures and metrics program is founded upon an established and clearly communicated set of internal controls focused on the integrity of the data that are gathered, the quality of the analysis and assessment applied to that data and the assurance of data protection. The consequences of failing to embed these principles within your metrics program will go directly to the credibility of the security program and its management.

It is important for us as individual business leaders to develop metrics programs in our organizations, not just because it is good for business and security, but because outside forces will eventually step in to do it for you. Take the initiative. You will see the results in the quality of security's connection to the business.

Good metrics tell a story

I am constantly hunting for metrics examples, and I am intrigued by the variety of ways experienced organizations present data. One vital measure of good data is its ability to inform and drive action in a specified direction.

---

[1] The upper right corner of the *Wall Street Journal* was typically used to highlight a company involved in some sort of wrongdoing.

Consider news organizations like the *Wall Street Journal*, which convert reams of data into meaningful copy that reveals a message to knowledgeable, time-challenged readers daily. Or think about medical lab work—next time you have a physical, ask for a copy of your blood work results and see if you can determine your health quotient. Sure, there are a few we have all memorized, like the bad this or the good that. But it is typically line after line of unintelligible gobbledygook—really important gobbledygook.

Your senior management and board members follow, absorb, and make crucial business decisions based on a host of spreadsheets, graphs, and trend lines. What kind of decisions would they make from gobbledygook?

I work with a variety of companies who have their own approach to data presentation. Frequently it focuses on timekeeping activities and incidents per whatever—per month, per shift, per quarter. These are data we must maintain to plan and manage, but I have beat the drum on many occasions about the limitations of counting things rather than analyzing our hard-earned data so that we may inform and influence.

We often forget that our typical customer does not see the data we present through anything remotely close to a level of informed judgment. They are disturbed by the trend that shows a 21% increase in workplace violence at Plant X, but do we leave them to draw their own conclusions on the root cause of these events? There has to be a story here that drives judgment and moves action.

Good metrics demand a story. The story reveals the lesson, the learning from the conclusions drawn by analysis of the data. Like any good story, you have to know your audience and select your theme to connect with their frame of reference. In the Plant X workplace violence example, analysis reveals a prevalence of alcohol use on the night shift with an obvious lack of supervisory oversight. In drilling down, it becomes clear that shift supervisors, security, and Human Resources (HR) are unclear on roles and reporting, and there is a general absence of policy and protocols around workplace behavior. The security director builds a briefing around these well-founded conclusions and is able to engage HR, legal and plant management on solutions that subsequently reduces these incidents to near zero. The story told to top management not only demonstrates leadership in resolving a potentially serious set of risks, but establishes security's role as an effective collaborator and business partner.

Good metrics must convey reliable information. We may be tempted to look at our data and make gut conclusions. The result may reveal symptoms and miss root causes. The story then is substantially fiction rather than fact. Fiction is not a good thing in our business. Effective, actionable risk management requires disciplined analysis. We have the knowledge to understand the data we have gathered. Counting incidents covers the How Much, but we have the obligation to probe the What, Where, Why and How to construct those scripts that reliably inform and influence.

When you look at your incident data for the past several months, what themes emerge? Pick a trend and drill down. What are the common denominators? How many of these risk events were preventable? What vulnerabilities contributed to their occurrence? What few cost-effective actions will most impact improvements?

Now tell me the story.

The Basics

Introduction

Members of corporate security organizations have long sought a catalog of metrics or measures they can use to reliably quantify the value that they bring to the enterprise they serve. It is all too easy for companies to primarily focus on quarterly earnings, department budget runs, and certain incident statistics. Unfortunately, many corporate security managers fail to utilize or even recognize the volumes of data their operations generate. Yet, these data may be captured and organized to produce a rich array of performance assessment tools that show value equal to quarterly earnings.

This book provides a variety of organizational measurements, concepts, metrics, indicators, and other criteria that may be employed to structure measures and metrics program models appropriate to the reader's specific operations and corporate sensitivities. This book is intended to stimulate thought on what might be effective within your unique business or organizational environment. Our focus is to briefly touch on multiple measures and metrics because there are so many options available. Ideally, this book will enable you to find one example that can be modified to accommodate your needs better than another. Future versions of this book will encompass examples of best practices that are identified as the field continues to grow.

CAVEAT EMPTOR!

Security metrics are not about numbers; they are about performance. Unless you have the intestinal fortitude to adequately plan and execute a program to legitimately measure how well specific security programs are delivering on their objectives—and stand the heat from the answers you may get—you likely are not going to benefit from this discussion. But your programs will be measured with or without you. Having the answers is just a good management.

Why measure, why metrics?

The fact that *established* metrics and measures for the full range of security programs are few and far between is due to the historical disconnection of these functions from the core businesses they serve. Businesses have historically used measures and metrics to evaluate performance, but not applied them to security practices. The risk environment has changed significantly over the past thirty years, and we have seen shocking wake-up calls to CEOs, boards, and shareholders. Attentive corporations now rely on more sophisticated and mainstream corporate security organizations to address risk exposure. With this mainstreaming comes the need (obligation) to measure performance as a way to demonstrate security's contribution to the bottom line. Metrics are a natural descendant of this process. Ultimately, there is no one to answer "Why measure, why metrics?" Each company will have its own answer or combination of answers. Some examples of potential answers (or frameworks) follow.

A gauge

Metrics can be a gauge on a company's dashboard. In fact, it is essential that we recognize security's contribution to the corporate system of internal controls. Internal controls are established to mitigate business risks. They comprise a dashboard that informs management on the status of core activities, allowing management to apply the brakes when needed to keep the enterprise safely on course. In providing a gauge or warning light on this dashboard, the security organization plays a critical role in identifying, measuring, preventing, and responding to a growing inventory of risks. When we identify a risk, we must be able to measure the probability and potential consequences of its occurrence so that management has a gauge to assess and prioritize what actions to take. Performance measurement and related metrics are central to understanding the adequacy of security controls and where to focus our limited resources for the greatest contribution to the protection strategy.

Accountability

Those involved in security management must be able to answer the question, "How secure are we?" or "When you last assessed our security posture on risk x or y, where did we stand?" This is where security organizations can show their accountability. It is about understanding where we were at a certain point in time and where we are now, given comparable metrics. We must also be able to show what we have done to move those metrics in our favor or why we have not succeeded in mitigating the risk or improving performance. Security organizations face accountability, and those guided by security policies and tools are accountable as well. When things go awry and risk is exposed, we are all measured one way or another.

Value center

More than ever, a security organization needs to be a value center, not just a cost center. The influence and value of a security organization is directly proportionate to its measurable impact on the ability of the enterprise to manage and mitigate the risk. Here is the value equation. Security adds value when its programs enable the business to be more productive (i.e., profitable).

A basic formula looks like this:

$$Security + business\ programs - risk = company\ profit.$$

A scorecard

How well is the security organization performing? You can pretty much rely on the fact that management is keeping a scorecard on the security function. Security organizations are measured every day, incident by incident or by a lack of incidents! It is advisable to make certain the measures used are the ones you know that are effective in accurately capturing your organization's success. Take the initiative to develop, sell, and deliver your own measures.

The business case

Are you prepared to answer the question: "How much less risk do I buy with what you are requesting here?" or, "What does security cost the company by each cost center or dollar of revenue?" What is the cost of security for specific assets? How do these costs impact our margins or our position with given products in the marketplace? How do we justify that expense and the additional resources we need to address new threats and initiatives? How do we answer the pundit who asks, "Let's take the risk that x won't happen?" Metrics provide grist for the probabilities, cost benefit, and cost effectiveness mills. By relying on hard data and providing measurable results, *they demonstrate that we understand the company's need to build a business case for resource commitment.*

Business alignment

Is security in your company an accepted part of the business? The business operations that security is chartered to protect seemingly live or die on metrics. So, who let security organizations off the hook and decided they do not need metrics? Security programs gather volumes of data every day. When the right information is gathered, security programs generate unique and informative data that:

- will define *what*, *where*, *how*, and *why* the risk is occurring;
- will eliminate plausible denial by business management;
- emphasize their accountability for safeguarding assets in their custody[1];
- directly aid in measuring service quality and customer satisfaction;

---

[1] This notion of business unit custody is one that will be repeated throughout this book. Security sets the policy and provides the tools but day-to-day security oversight belongs in the neighborhood that owns, operates, and relies upon it.

- provide measurable support for new and existing programs; and
- clearly contribute to a variety of value-based assessments.

The successful security executive, manager, or supervisor defines their business plan and the performance of resources and services around clearly articulated measures. Those measures should be aligned with core business strategy and priorities.

THOUGHT QUESTIONS

- In your company, what security organization initiatives have enabled the business to successfully accomplish a business goal?
- Can you think of a business initiative that has risk that you understand but others may not?
- What could the security department do to help that initiative succeed?
- Are you adding value? You bet!

What are security metrics?

Essentially, metrics are a system of measurement. Security metrics are those that are applied to the field of security, to measure the effectiveness of security programs or functions put into place.

The Systems Security Engineering Capability Maturity Model (SSE-CMM), designed by Carnegie Mellon University, identifies the role of security metrics: "Security metrics focus on the actions...that organizations take to reduce and manage the risks...that arise when security defenses or protocols are breached."[2]

Corporate boards of directors, C-level management, and other stakeholders face challenging questions related to security metrics, which are identified in the SSE-CMM:

> *How much money should be spent on security?*
> *How much of a company's resources should be devoted to security?*
> *How are business components prioritized when deciding which to target first?*
> *How can the system be effectively configured?*
> *How much improvement is gained by security expenditures?*
> *How do we determine which improvements to security processes are needed?*
> *How do we measure the improvements?*
> *How do we measure whether we are reducing our exposure?[3]*

A casual Internet search for "security metrics" yields page after page of (often duplicative) sources keyed largely to the development of metrics around information security effectiveness. Certainly, the discipline and structure of these approaches are

---

[2] The Systems Security Engineering Capability Maturity Model (SSE-CMM), Carnegie Mellon University, 1995, www.sse-cmm.org/metric/metric.asp.
[3] Ibid.

recommended and useful to the larger scope of "corporate security." However, we are more interested here in providing a thought process around the data and potential measures that are available as daily outputs of the work of a broader portfolio of security services.

Corporate security has undergone a transition in boardroom visibility and status since the 9/11 terrorist attacks. Security executives increasingly seek information on measures and metrics that apply to their service portfolios because they appreciate the need for established performance measures. This book intends to help those who manage security programs leverage this new visibility, while stimulating thought and encouraging an exchange of ideas on security measures and metrics.

What are the components of a measures and metrics program?

There is no definitive configuration of components that comprise a standard security measures and metrics program. Each business will need to choose which measures and metrics apply to their own interests. However, there are some components that apply broadly to most companies.

The National Institute of Standards and Technology (NIST), a federal technology agency under the Department of Commerce, is devoted to U.S. industrial competitiveness in a global market. Table 1.1 provides definitions, created by the NIST, of components essential to an information security measures and metrics program. Incorporating these components is valuable in measuring information security, yet they are applicable to the broader field of security in general and would be useful in any program.[4]

As you can see, this NIST breakdown provides an excellent overview of what elements a security metrics program should contain. That is, a program should start with a *performance goal*. There should be a clear *purpose* for each metric. There need to be established *data sources* and *frequencies* to legitimize the metric. Identifiable *indicators* strengthen a metric program's elements and purposes. Of particular note in this table is the focus on security program performance measurement rather than the simple expression of a statistic.

What is "corporate security?" The need for a consolidated view of security measures

One of the key reasons security organizations have not been held to universal standards of measurement is that there is no established model for the corporate security

---

[4] "IT Security Metrics Guidance: A Practical Approach to Measuring Information Security," PowerPoint Presentation, Joan Hash and Tim Grace, National Institute of Standards and Technology, page 8.

Table 1.1 The National Institute of Standards and Technology's Features of a Measures and Metrics Program

Performance goal	Desired results of implementing one or several system security control objectives/techniques that are measured by the metric.
Performance objective	Actions that are required to accomplish the performance goal.
Metric	Quantitative measurement(s) provided by the metric.
Purpose	Overall functionality obtained by collecting the metric; whether the metric will be used for internal performance measurement or external reporting; what insights are hoped to be gained from the metric; regulatory or legal reasons for collecting a specific metric if such exist, or other similar items.
Implementation evidence	Proof of the security controls' existence that validates implementation. Implementation evidence is used to calculate the metric as indirect indicators that validate that the activity is performed and as causation factors that may point to the causes of unsatisfactory results for a specific metric.
Frequency	Time periods for collection of data.
Formula	Calculation to be performed that results in a numeric expression of a metric.
Data source	Location of the data to be used in calculating the metric.
Indicators	Information about the meaning of a metric and its performance trend; possible causes of trends; possible solutions to correct observed shortcomings; performance target if it has been set for the metric and indication of what trends would be considered positive in relation to the performance target.

---

organization.[5] Anyone can search for and find a suite of services typically assigned to a chief financial officer, a chief legal officer, a chief auditor, a chief risk officer, or almost any other senior governance executive. In addition, there is no set of typical assignments or responsibilities. Many corporations do not see the need to have the full range of security services available. They may perceive their organization to have a low-risk exposure and therefore have a resulting risk acceptance strategy. This creates a difficult situation for security executives who face a mandate to reduce the risk but are left without the authority or tools to do so. Relatively few chief security officers (CSOs) have all security-related services under one unified portfolio, although there is growing acceptance of this integrated approach. Where physical security and information security are linked, "convergence" is the current trend. However, this increasingly popular notion of an integrated security program is still far too narrow and excludes multiple elements of security services that are core to the protection of the enterprise. The range of security services is

---

[5] See the *Chief Security Officer—An Organizational Model,* ASIS International (2013), for an excellent discussion on a consolidated service model for the chief security officer.

connected regardless of where they are assigned on an organization chart. Consider the following:

- An effective, logical security program is dependent upon an equally effective physical security and business conduct program.
- There is a direct connection between the absence of a comprehensive background investigation program and instances of internal crime and misconduct.
- There is real risk in the failure to engage in effective technical and integrity-based due diligence where there is proposed engagement with outside vendors who have access to sensitive information or processes.
- Physical access and alarm control systems contribute directly to the ability for early identification of risk and proactive evacuation of facilities in emergency conditions.
- Demonstrated capabilities to proactively protect against a variety of insured risks contribute to lower insurance rates and contribution to the bottom line.
- A comprehensive security policy infrastructure supported by an effective security awareness program with the employee/manager population has a greater likelihood of lower incidents of internal crime and misconduct and more rapid and informed response to events that could harm the business and its employees.
- Qualified first responders within a security organization see potential hazards in information security, business continuity, and other areas from a unique perspective in time and focus.
- All forms of investigation of incidents resulting in financial and/or reputational loss offer opportunities to identify or reaffirm known vulnerabilities that must be closed to avoid future risk.

When security professionals fail to be inclusive and respectful of other people's competencies and contributions to enterprise security, it detracts from the quality of protection our companies deserve. If you think this is wrong, you have been listening to yourself for too long.

Operational excellence: the business context for metrics

The delivery of excellence in a business' products or services has always been a widely accepted objective. But expectations took on a more formalized agenda in the 1980s, culminating with the Baldrige National Quality Award that was set as a standard of excellence for U.S. business.[6] Global competition in manufacturing spawned several disciplines targeting continuous improvement, defect elimination, cost management, supply chain efficiency, and the customer/value relationship. In sum, these and their companions in the pursuit of quality-driven operational performance can all be placed in a bucket labeled "Business Excellence." If enterprise security is to be effectively aligned with its company's strategy and processes, it must be driving a focus on operations excellence into every corner of its suite of products and services.

---

[6] See http://www.nist.gov/baldrige/ for more information about this award.

The business context for metrics has to be fundamentally grounded on a foundation of operational excellence. When we build our programs for a clear connection to performance excellence in mitigating risk and serving the goals of the enterprise, our value is far more visible and measurable. But how should we—our stakeholders *and* ourselves—define excellence in corporate security's suite of services? Is it in the quality of program results and, if so, where are the established standards to measure a requisite degree of quality? At the end of the day, customers define quality and value. The "owner" of the security process cannot be the sole arbiter of its level of quality and excellence. But it is also true that the security function is not the sole contributor to a secure business process. It is a shared accountability with degrees of contribution linked to the requirements of protection. Clearly, engaging stakeholders and customers in analysis of our activities is an essential ingredient in the process. Our customers do not typically understand security activities, and a well-planned examination of what service excellence means to them will make activity analysis and measurement more effective and more valuable.

Is a "best practice" equal to excellence in that practice? Where a security practice can be shown to deliver results consistently superior to an alternative process that has been applied and tested by others, it should be advertised as having achieved a level of excellence. The key is measuring the "superior results," and that requires detailed task and process analyses, which are consistent elements in virtually all business excellence disciplines.

If a security process or activity lacks established performance measures, can excellence be achieved in that process or activity? It is not possible to establish that a security process has achieved excellence or provided value if relevant performance measures have not been vetted and consistently applied.

Probing potential measures of excellence in security programs

What statements might sufficiently convey a demonstration of excellence in security programs? Consider the following:

- A security program demonstrates such effective alignment and contribution to the success of a business process that it measurably enables the business to do what would otherwise be too risky or noncompetitive. Moreover, business is captured and/or retained solely due to the quality of security measures proposed or applied.
- Measurable capabilities in safe and secure workplace protection result in increased productivity, lower insurance cost, increased worker morale, and reduced incidence of injury and fatality.
- A security activity is peer reviewed or benchmarked against available standards or best practices and *exceeds* qualitative measures of performance. Certain control factors being equal, losses attributable to security breach are measurably less (over time) than industry sector peers.
- The cost of a secure business process or environment is less than the consequences of risk or, the cost is additive but those at risk feel measurably safer and

more productive. Or, an incremental increase in asset protection is achieved at reduced cost to the customer.

- A customer's expectation (or service level agreement) is consistently and measurably exceeded.

If a process has not already been identified for analysis and application of an established program within your company, you may want to consider Table 1.2 as a team exercise. Each of the security programs and services may be discussed, evaluated, and selected for the potential benefits that may accrue as a result of an in-depth application of an operations excellence approach. Several items in the table have been highlighted and noted (+/++) where an added benefit may be found through subsequent analysis. The idea is to think through how each of the possible benefits on the left may impact and deliver measurable results to the security service targeted.

The balanced scorecard[7]

The conceptual framework of operational excellence may also be found in the balanced scorecard, which has been a frequently cited example of an operational measurement approach to business performance that could also be evaluated for adoption in security management. There are four focal points (or quadrants) to the scorecard that may be translated for our purposes as follows:

1. The financial perspective: What goals and measures in safety, security, integrity, or other safeguards are perceptible to security's stakeholders? These perceptions also drive the critical objective of employee awareness and accountability.
2. The internal business perspective: What goals and measures in our key protection programs demonstrate best-in-class practices? As noted above, measurable results drive an assessment of superior performance.
3. The innovation and learning perspective: What goals and measures are calculated to improve security at reduced cost and thereby add value? Reducing specific risks with measurably effective security programs also may be seen as an adding value.
4. The customer perspective: What security goals and measures will contribute to customer satisfaction and our ability to deliver value to them?

The idea here is to link these key perspectives to your consideration of the objectives and measures that will drive security's performance in these quadrants of business management. These are not trivial concepts. Security executives too often fail to focus on measuring (and reporting) on their programs' cost and definable value and the essential requirement to connect those programs to their customer's needs. The demonstration of best in class invariably imposes a body of key performance metrics and indicators as evidence of quantifiable excellence.

---

[7]"The balanced scorecard—Measures that drive performance," Robert Kaplan and David Norton, *Harvard Business Review,* Reprint no.92105, January–February, 1992.

Table 1.2 Analysis of Security Programs and Services

Contribution from Examination of Relevant Business Excellence Factors	Security Programs and Services											
	Manage the Business for Results	Align Security with Business Objectives	Establish and Promote a Culturally Responsive Policy Framework	Assess Risk and Develop Measurably Responsive Mitigation Plans	Focus Protection on Critical Assets and Processes	Provide for Timely and Qualitative Incident Response	Provide Safe and Secure Workplace	Obtain Business-Responsive Results from Investigations	Screen Employees and Vendors for Integrity	Anticipate Crises and Provide for Business Continuity	Protect Information	Assure Customer Awareness of Risk
Deliver measurable contribution to business objectives	+	‡		+	+		‡			‡	‡	
Notable improvement in knowledge of emerging risk				‡	‡			+				‡
Notable benefit from improved customer involvement in security tasks		‡		‡	+	‡				‡	‡	+
Improved responsiveness to key risk indicators	+			‡	+	+				‡	‡	‡
Notable benefit from continuous process improvement	+			‡	‡				+		‡	
Improved alignment with key performance indicators				‡	+	+		‡				

Table 1.2 Analysis of Security Programs and Services—cont'd

Availability of comparable best-in-class security practices		+						+	‡
Ability to perform activity-based task analysis and costing				‡			+	‡	‡
Notable benefit from process defect identification and elimination	+		‡		+	‡	‡	‡	‡
Benefit from reduced cycle time				‡	‡	‡	‡		
Availability and reliability of measurements and metrics	+		‡		‡	+	+		‡
Measurable improvement in essential knowledge			‡					‡	
Notable benefit from improved training and employee involvement			‡		‡	‡	+		‡

The risk management context for metrics

Consider this: *It is only because there are unacceptable risks that the cost of a security program is tolerated.* Risk management is the process of identifying and understanding applicable risks and taking informed actions to reduce potential failure, achieve business objectives, and decrease business performance uncertainty. There are four categories of risk currently confronting businesses:

1. Strategic risk: These risks are an inherent part of the business environment and have a significant effect on revenues, earnings, market share, and product offerings.
2. Organizational risk: These risks are part of a business unit's environment, relating to people, politics, and values that can impact organizational effectiveness.
3. Financial risk: These are market, credit, and liquidity risks that create uncertainty, exposure to loss, and the potential that the business will not be able to meet its future obligations.
4. Operational risk: These are risks of loss from inadequate system controls, human error, or other management failure. These areas have increasingly become a part of security's realm, encompassing fraud, data integrity, risky operating environments, information security, business continuity, inadequate policies and controls, and the rich variety of standard personnel problems.[8]

Metrics in these arenas abound because we need to know where to devote scarce resources to their management. Corporations spend millions in measuring, anticipating, preparing, and responding to their implications. If we are able to manage these risk categories well, we can reduce the likelihood of their occurrence or at least minimize their impact.

THOUGHT QUESTIONS

- Is security in your enterprise clearly placed in the risk management family of corporate services?
- If yes, what benefits are offered as a result?
- If not, what do you think has been lost in terms of your ability to impact the potential consequences of security-related risks?

The regulatory context for metrics

Security no longer enjoys the cover of executive ignorance and inattention. Look at any number of corporate and natural disasters and see how politicians protect their

---

[8] With the exception of passing mentions of information security, business continuity, and fraud, it is unfortunate that reviews of risk management journals, websites, and texts almost universally fail to find a comprehensive treatment of security-related risks.

seats and insurance companies protect their pocketbooks in terms of risk mitigation. And yet, as a society we are predominantly reactive rather than proactive. Historically, the majority of our fire laws followed the 1942 Cocoanut Grove nightclub fire in Boston. Likewise, Executive Order 13224 (blocking terrorist property and assets), Chemical Facility Anti-Terrorism Standards, Customs-Trade Partnership Against Terrorism, the TSA HAZMAT Endorsement Threat Assessment Program, and the Maritime Transportation Security Act were all in response to the 9/11 attacks. And the Sarbanes–Oxley Act came on the heels of the Enron scandal (and others). Even our current privacy and information security regulations were enacted after a flood of identity thefts.

Regulators and insurance carriers consistently apply measures and metrics; for example, a communication from an insurance provider might read: "As you can see from the attached schedule, we are 63% in compliance and will complete the balance of our security enhancements within the next 240 days." The numbers in the example would be based on measurable data. Typically, security-related regulations also require risk assessments that are measurable (see the FDA's CARVER + Shock risk-assessment tool in Chapter 2); security enhancements or indications of the degree of current compliance that are measurable; time and cost to comply that is measurable; and schedules and other indicators of conformance to the letter and spirit of the legislation.

THOUGHT QUESTIONS

- What security, integrity, or other related regulations or insurance requirements have emerged for your business(es)?
- Was there a security organization involved in the response and follow-up procedures?
- What did you learn from this experience that you could pass on?

The CSO's context for metrics

It pays to advertise. That is, it pays to advertise our own services so that the value of those services is kept front and center. Those readers who are CSOs, may get caught up in being responsive and forget that they are really in the education business. In fact, everyone in charge of, or invested in security is in the education business. Put more bluntly, we need to empower (with information) those in the company who fully understand the value of security metrics and eliminate plausible deniability from those who do not. We have to continually drive home the notion of business unit responsibility, meaning that security is ensured when the employees of each business unit exercise knowledgeable oversight. Where correctly focused, measures and metrics are pointedly informative and enable our constituents to see the results of measurably effective and ineffective security initiatives. In the wake of corporate meltdowns caused by the ethically deficient, this educational focus needs to reach to the board of directors and across the ranks of senior corporate management.

Security executives must know how to influence the corporate population and business focus

There are five key pillars in a measurably influential security program:

1. A framework of security policies explicitly endorsed by top management to provide the legal framework for positive influence.
2. A core management philosophy that holds line managers accountable for protecting the firm and establishes the security executive as the content expert prepared to empower those managers with the information they need to be effective custodians.
3. A clearly established role in the firm's risk management program that enables the security executive to better understand the adequacy of business process controls and to influence the governance infrastructure on lessons learned.
4. A qualitative analysis and reporting program that provides the metrics dashboard, connects the dots, and draws actionable conclusions.
5. A comprehensive communication and awareness program that provides the script for influence and employee empowerment.

It is generally accepted that the truly effective executive is the one who has mastered the ability to influence both up and down the corporate ladder in their organization. Influence as a core competency is also at the heart of the measurably effective CSO. Metrics are a tool used to facilitate influence; to demonstrate, argue, support, and convince.

The legal context: the critical value of a policy infrastructure

As stated above, the foundation of an effective corporate security program is a high-level policy infrastructure accepted by top management and the board. It is the rulebook, the legal framework for the program. The Business Roundtable's *CEO Guide to Security Challenges*[9] summed it this way: "The CEO is ultimately responsible for a corporation's security culture and policies. Hence, a CEO should articulate a clear statement of expectations for security throughout the corporation. Line managers should then devise ways to implement those expectations and report back to the CEO on goals, programs and metrics. Performance metrics can be created to evaluate whether or not the corporate security expectations are being met."

It would seem likely (or at least we would hope) that an informed CEO with a concern for security could embrace each of the following brief policy statements:

• The highest standard of integrity and ethical behavior is the foundation of this corporation. In support of this principle, corporate security will investigate allegations of criminal activity and unethical business conduct and will maintain a proactive program of crime prevention and asset protection.
• We will maintain safe and secure workplaces for our employees and invitees.

---

[9]*Committed to Protecting America: CEO Guide to Security Challenges,* February, 2005, Business Roundtable, 1615 L Street NW, Suite 1100, Washington, DC 20036, page 10.

- The corporation's sensitive, private information and processes will be aggressively protected throughout the information life cycle and for all information media.
- Access to the corporation's facilities, information, and systems will be based on clearly articulated business requirements.
- Business relationships that may present risk to the corporation and/or our customers will be proactively examined to identify substantive issues of concern.
- Persons found to have verifiable and significant derogatory background histories will not be employed nor allowed access to our premises, information, or systems.
- We will ensure that every manager plans for emergencies that may affect the safety of our employees or interrupt our critical business processes.
- Corporate security will analyze and communicate risk-related information to business units to raise awareness and recommend appropriate action.

In addition to providing a core set of expectations that frame roles and responsibilities, each of these policy statements can be translated to an actionable, *measurable* set of activities. The policy is the high-level requirement or goal, but it needs an implementation framework such as the examples shown in Table 1.3. The implementation framework includes a standard, procedure, guideline, and metric, all of which are derived from and support the policy statement.

At the end of the day, the business context for metrics is the only reference point you need. Make a connection as to how *valued* the metrics and measures are that are used in your business culture. Find the few senior managers who do it well and learn from them. Find and use the few metrics that clearly demonstrate how the security organization is helping your company to be less at risk and, as a result, more competitive.

THOUGHT QUESTIONS

- Do you have a core set of security policies that have been approved by top management and communicated to all appropriate personnel?
- If not, what do you think is lacking in the effectiveness of your security program?
- How do you measure conformance to those policies?
- Based on a frequency of risk-related incidents, is there a demonstrated need for a policy and associated framework to address this exposure?

Opening exercise: what is the *real* cost of security in your company?

If you do not have a clue about this metric, now would be a good time to learn what it is. This exercise assumes that the reader is in an organization where security is on the enterprise agenda, but even for those where a protection program is only dimly lit, it can be revealing.

Table 1.3 Examples of Measurable Activities for Policy Statements

Policy	The corporation's sensitive, private information and processes will be aggressively protected throughout the information life cycle and for all information media.
Standard	All documents will be classified in accordance with their sensitivity to compromise. Approved classifications are: highly confidential, confidential, internal, and public.
Procedure	Every page of a classified document will be visibly labeled in the footer.
Guideline	Discussion of classified information should only be with those who have a business need to know and never in public places or via cell phones.
Metric	Percent of sampled documents in business unit X that are appropriately labeled this assessment period vs last.

Why is it important to understand this metric? Put quite simply, when the real cost of security becomes a known quantity, you will learn where some of the skeletons are buried, find both detractors and supporters for good security, and understand a lot more about how to tie the pieces together for a more coordinated, focused, and effective program. You will also be armed with a metric that likely nobody else has (and perhaps one you will want to keep close at hand). This exercise is both one of disciplined investigation and best guesswork. The central rule is that you need to define "security and corporate protection" broadly. Business continuity may not be a program that others would ascribe to "security" but think about the notion of proactive protection and crisis response and the breadth of resources devoted to address these issues. As for costing various elements (see Table 1.4), find generic categories of labor rates for both salaried (exempt) and hourly (nonexempt) internal staff and annual contract amounts for services and products.

In many global companies there is a growing tendency to have security guard coverage outsourced and reporting to local facility management. These costs can be large, but because they are decentralized there is a resulting loss of total cost awareness to the enterprise. A security director with indirect responsibility should make a concentrated effort to identify all guard costs and focus on opportunities to improve cost management.

Table 1.4 shows just a few examples of time commitments associated with the administration of a security program within a modern enterprise. Where security-related responsibilities are spread among several departments without some consolidated oversight, costs tend to be masked and accountability can be diluted. But the real costs are found in the day-to-day tasks carried out by the company's employees, vendors, visitors, and others that are rarely calculated for impact analysis. You would do well to identify these tasks and tally the costs.

THOUGHT QUESTIONS

- If you were able to do this exercise, what were the results and your reaction to them?
- How could this information be useful to you?
- Who would you be least likely to share it with? Why?
- Can you itemize some expenses that could be eliminated or efficiencies obtained through better coordination and planning?

Table 1.4 Calculating the Cost of Security	
Cost Element	**Est. $**
1. *Direct security expenses*: Enter the annual budget for the current year security program.	
2. *Indirect security expenses*: Obtain where possible or estimate the time, materials, and other expenses associated with security-related activities by nonsecurity personnel. Examples are (some of these may be considered direct depending on the organizational model employed):	
a. Fire prevention, life safety, and code-related equipment, systems, and programs typically budgeted in facility costs.	
b. HR or other time related to background investigations (and reinvestigations).	
c. Internal and external criminal and misconduct investigations to include all probative, analytical, travel, data search, equipment purchase/leasing, interview time of employees, or billable vendor/contractor time.	
d. Business unit staff time engaged in risk analyses and other activities associated with understanding the security risk environment. Include employee time engaged in security-related awareness, training, and professional development, including time of consultant brought in for special programs.	
e. Annual purchases of security-related subscription services (software, online, and hard copy), sensing, monitoring, compliance (Sarbanes–Oxley), control, and reporting subsystems to include those associated with physical and information security and investigative tools not budgeted by corporate security.	
f. Internal and contractual expenses related to the due diligence vetting of third-party contractors for integrity, security requirements, financial and legal assurance, and other reliability standards.	
g. Time of internal and external audit staff assigned to security-related examinations.	
h. Cost of losses, business unit downtime to failed safeguards, security-related fines, injury from known hazards, etc.	
i. Capital (construction/renovation) expenses related to new space protection fit up and special features such as those associated with regulatory or ordinance compliance.	
j. Estimated annual time of legal, finance, oversight executives, and other key interdependencies to address issues brought to them by security elements.	
k. Time of line business and contract personnel to develop, update, maintain, and test business continuity and crisis management plans.	
l. Physical and logical access: Cost per person for processing new staff and contractors for access to facilities and computing applications.	
m. Daily average time of each employee to address physical access, system log-in, and other administratively imposed security procedures times average of 220 days per year.	
n. Indirect security expenses: Identify the activities that serve to support corporate protection such as equipment and software purchase capitalization expenses.	
o. Other (list)	
Total	

Good metrics are SMART

The remaining sections of this book will briefly discuss and give examples of metrics that we think will prove applicable and useful to the reader. A message worth repeating is that an inventory of several hundred metrics and measures is meant to be a warehouse, not a data dump. Collected data must be both predictive and actionable. Otherwise, your company is no better off for having collected it.

One reason for the insistence that data be predictive is that there are far too many metrics out there. According to *chief financial officer* magazine, in an article looking at the reasons why balanced scorecards fail, research by The Hackett Group found that "the average senior executive is inundated with 132 metrics (83 financial and 49 operational) every month. That is nearly nine times more than the number of measures landing on the desks of senior executives at best practice companies."[10]

Keep the caution of being *SMART* with your metrics and you will find measurable ways to inform and influence your constituents. SMART metrics are Specific, Measurable, Attainable, Relevant, and Timely (Figure 1.1).

Keep your measures and metrics in proper perspective

Because "corporate security" is implemented in so many different ways with such disparate resources, it is impossible to develop this book for just one audience. Rather, we hope it offers value to a variety of individuals interested in the administration of a security program.

We are aware that many users will have few, if any, dedicated staff to assign to the maintenance of a metrics program. But to suggest that a security executive or manager need not maintain a set of key measures on his or her programs belies the growing number of clearly successful and influential CSOs. These successful CSOs

SPECIFIC	Metrics are specific and target the area you are measuring.
MEASURABLE	You can collect data that is accurate and complete.
ATTAINABLE	The metrics are easy to understand, and it is clear when you chart your performance over time which direction is "good" and which direction is "bad."
RELEVANT	Do not measure things that are not important.
TIMELY	You can get the data when you need it and it is current for responsive action.

FIGURE 1.1

SMART metrics.

Derived from W. Wesner et al., Winning with Quality, *Addison-Wesley, 1995.*

---

[10] Janet Kersnar, "Swamped: Why Do Balanced Scorecards Fail?" November 16, 2004, *CFO,* http://ww2.cfo.com/strategy/2004/11/swamped/.

measure that which tells them how well their security processes are working and those things that are important to their constituents. They do not waste precious time collecting and massaging data simply because it is there. They pick the few metrics that matter and reach out to a motivated assistant or someone in another department who can help them with organizing and presenting the data.

Making the book work for you

This book is meant to be a collaborative work in progress. We want it to grow along with our readers' learning. New threats and risks are presented with increasing frequency and so are the solutions and how we measure them. Because there is such variety in corporate security programs, this book is meant to stimulate ideas and thoughtful reflection on examples that work for you.

THOUGHT QUESTIONS

- What would a fully integrated security program under a single chief security office look like in your organization?
- What issues or constraints make this unfeasible?
- How would you characterize the benefits that would accrue to such a model?

Types of Metrics and Performance Indicators Appropriate to the Security Mission

2

The inventory of metrics and measurable performance indicators are so broad and diverse that it is a challenge to find those that fit for multiple purposes. We work within organizational settings that experiment and apply performance measurement and improvement programs in various iterations, so it is important to identify some of the more popular ones. Suffice it to say that quantitative measures are everywhere, in whatever business you are in and it remains for you to find those that serve your purposes to the best advantage or, at a minimum, understand what is about to happen to you. The following information attempts to set forth those measures with the greatest staying power and those we have found that tend to best serve our unique (and often misunderstood) missions. You will also find several hundred examples of measures and metrics in Appendix 1. They have been organized into categories of security services to allow for customization to suit the reader's operational needs.

Influential initiatives from the corner office

There are several quality/productivity/business-process improvement initiatives that set the stage for our security metrics considerations. They focus on elimination of defects, customer satisfaction, and best practices and have significant traction in many corporations. They all have a central component of measurement and comparative metrics. As a service function, we are invariably drawn into these initiatives (though sometimes kicking and screaming). But, aside from corporate survival, there are compelling reasons to learn and apply the notion of process improvement. Five key processes are briefly highlighted here, though there are many others available.

Key performance indicators

Key performance indicators (KPIs) refer to the organization's critical success factors and aid in defining and measuring progress toward goals. KPIs provide those measurements. Utilizing KPIs involves setting target performance levels and measuring progress or variance on a periodic basis. The notion of the "executive dashboard" to provide performance metrics at a glance has gained some popularity in the literature and with software programs. The security executive's dashboard would likely track such indicators as progress toward process improvement (e.g., reduce guard force overtime by 15% in the first quarter) or risk reduction (e.g., reduce laptop thefts in the regional center complex by 50% by the end of Q2).

ISO series

The previous chapter spoke briefly to operational excellence and its relevance to performance quality. Additionally, the International Organization for Standardization (ISO) 9000 series provides international assurance that a company has formalized its quality management systems and may be used as an integral part of their internal control framework within shared space with other governance functions. ISO 31000 is a codified framework of risk management principles that apply directly to corporate security's enterprise risk management mission although our influence in terms of scope is ominously absent. Having said that, our colleagues from the information security ranks do have established ownership and engagement in the ISO 27000 series. A company that takes the pains to qualify for ISO certification deserves to have its asset protection programs within this envelope of quality and program performance standards. Performance measures and metrics are at the core of these credentials, and security programs can be a risk management and profit-centered component of these initiatives. It is likely that you can find resources within your company that are applying these methodologies and can advise on potential applications within the broader scope of corporate-wide security operations.

Six Sigma

Six Sigma is a highly structured, data-driven methodology focused on cost, quality, and schedule/cycle time keyed to customer expectations that clearly resides within the operational excellence framework. The objective of the methodology is the implementation of a customer-focused, measurement-based strategy that centers on in-depth process analysis, defect identification/reduction and quantifiable service delivery improvement. Familiarize yourself with the process but do not pursue this methodology if you do not have the staff time or consultant support to generate the numbers to accurately measure both current state and proposed improvement. If you have the resources within your quality organization or elsewhere and the time to devote to the process, there are many metric-based benefits to Six Sigma that are worth exploring. If you put your risk manager hat on, explore Six Sigma as an approach to disciplined vulnerability analysis centered on defects: Why did protection break down? What are the causes of safeguard failure? What is the likelihood of future risk, the *measurable* criticality of asset(s) and cost-effectiveness trade-offs of alternative countermeasures?

Benchmarking

Benchmarking is a typical form of comparative assessment that has both advantages and limitations. In its more business-centered application, it is far more involved, structured, and costly than engaging in some friendly web-based surveys among colleagues. Because benchmarking focuses on similar processes, it need not be employed among comparative (i.e., security) applications. Actionable results tend to be highly metric-oriented to permit transferability for program modification. As noted in Table 2.1 below, the general absence of a body of best practices tends to limit benchmarking in some security programs.

Except when clearly severe and immediate risk is overwhelmingly evident to top management and shareholders, the security organization will almost always be a target of cost management and containment. Often, outside consultants who specialize in efficiency studies and related cost-reduction engagements are blindly focused on numbers, sometimes even if the numbers fail to support their starting line assumptions. The business-centered and proactive security executive will have (1) demonstrated over time how specific security services provide measurable outputs to core business functions, and (2) identified a set of key metrics and conclusions to inform senior management with *actionable data* on risk mitigation tactics taken by the security organization and recommended for affected business units. This will help the security organization avoid being a target of cost containment initiatives.

Figure 2.1 shows an example of a simple benchmarking exercise among a dozen colleagues in a specific industrial sector.

These results are so striking that further analysis is essential. It turns out that the sponsoring CSO (#1) in this figure has virtually eliminated all fixed security posts

Table 2.1 Pros and Cons of Benchmarking

Benchmarking	
Pros	**Cons**
Identifies best practices to enable creating a baseline for existing security services and processes.	While it is growing, relatively little data exists on what is a "common or best security practice." Moreover, it is very difficult to find two security organizations that have comparable programs.
Very useful for competitive analysis particularly where the results indicate favorable data.	Benchmarking exercises are time consuming and potentially very expensive.
Provides a credible, proven platform for change that can offer justification for resources.	Security processes may be difficult to replicate in a different security environment.
Pushes traditional thinking "out of the box" where senior management is truly behind the process.	It is often (justifiably) difficult to engage partners, especially competitors where valued.
Likely would receive kudos from senior management who would see effort for improvement.	You may not like the results! Be prepared to really challenge your assumptions on programs.
If a disciplined process, you will learn details you did not know about the cost and performance of some activities.	See above. Be careful what you ask for, you may get it.

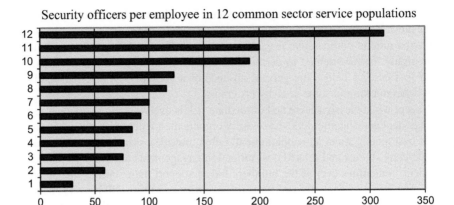

FIGURE 2.1

Benchmarking security officer-to-employee ratio.

after installing a reliable electronic access control system and implementing a corporate-wide access control policy. Those respondents in the upper numbers continue to extensively employ these fixed security officer posts. The cost implications of these results are equally striking. Headcount, whether yours or contracted, is costly and in this case the sponsoring CSO is clearly demonstrating a value while also providing a return on investment (ROI) on the access control system which has been depreciated over several years. The information presented in the figure shows a similar trend for each respondent and reinforces the cost efficiency of those in the lower security headcount. An important caution in this example is to ask about the degree to which each of the programs in the sample is truly comparable. Does company #12, for example, have a significant number of entry points that management has said should be staffed with a security presence?

A simple presentation like this can very clearly demonstrate to higher management cost efficiency in a known universe in very responsive ways. Moreover, given the anonymity of the benchmarking exercise and security's lower profile, it will not end up coming back to haunt those respondents who are sustaining the higher costs, yet they might learn from the results when shared.

Service level agreements[1]

Service level agreements (SLA) are often found between internal service organizations and their customer business units. The CSO should consider the value of managing expectations within these agreements between security and key internal

---

[1] Some IT security literature begins to explore the notion of Protection Level Agreements and Quality of Protection (QoP) standards. Providing guarantees on levels of protection is likely a very hazardous venture in our business but deserves a thorough examination in several areas including IT security, business recovery, response time, process cycle times, etc.

customers. Where applied externally with vendors, they need to be more contractually binding though the focus on performance is the same; SLAs typically contain performance tracking and reporting requirements with embedded benchmarks and metrics to be employed. Cycle times for specific deliverables, turnover rates for guard services, and response times are typical examples. The use of metrics in the scope of services definition requires the supplier to thoroughly understand his abilities to meet specified standards (both cost and performance) on a consistent basis.

THOUGHT QUESTIONS

- Have any of these or other "corner office initiatives" landed on your doorstep?
- Did they contribute to security's elevation or reduction in visibility or influence? Why?
- Did your function(s) have the metrics readily available to support your contributions to corporate health?
- What could better demonstrate the value of your services and support retention of current resources?

The CSO dashboard

Every CSO should have half a dozen dials that are watched on a regular basis. These indicators could be "survival metrics"—the hot buttons you are expected to address or those few dials that monitor selected wellness indicators unique to your organization or of particular concern to management (Figure 2.2). For example, if you are in financial services, you might be particularly attuned to the number of business units with dated contingency plans and inadequate software patch administration, internal misconduct or numbers of people hired with known derogatory backgrounds. Your business may be in hostile locations or be increasingly dependent on third parties you know have poor security controls. What if you are concerned that your security service vendor is giving you increasing numbers of problematic personnel? Each of us can select a few key metrics we should watch because they are the things that keep us awake at night. You may find that you have more than one dashboard—yours and the one(s) your boss and a few key others expect you to watch and report on. The chief financial officer (CFO) may be an excellent resource to advise on the presentation of dashboard metrics since this officer typically reports performance metrics to management on a regular basis. Look for some meters or dials in the following discussions that can serve to improve or develop your dashboard.

THOUGHT QUESTIONS

- What dashboard do you currently employ and how would you rate its acceptance by your targeted constituents?
- What three or four dials most directly impact your management's perception of your success? Are they the right ones in your view?
- If not, how would you set them straight?

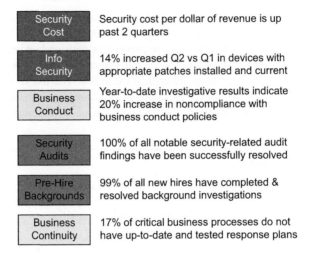

Security Cost	Security cost per dollar of revenue is up past 2 quarters
Info Security	14% increased Q2 vs Q1 in devices with appropriate patches installed and current
Business Conduct	Year-to-date investigative results indicate 20% increase in noncompliance with business conduct policies
Security Audits	100% of all notable security-related audit findings have been successfully resolved
Pre-Hire Backgrounds	99% of all new hires have completed & resolved background investigations
Business Continuity	17% of critical business processes do not have up-to-date and tested response plans

FIGURE 2.2

Security dashboard metrics. (For color version of this figure, the reader is referred to the online version of this book.)

Risk analyses

Risk analyses are compulsory exercises performed on a periodic basis and offer what is perhaps the most useful and critical information for performance assessment. They offer significant opportunities to test current assumptions about threats and their likelihood, proactively identify vulnerabilities to these threats, confirm the effectiveness of existing security measures, and offer opportunities to challenge current assumptions on alternative approaches to asset protection. Keep in mind that in the risk management inventory, we in security largely live within the operational or service delivery risk framework, rather than a theoretical framework. You should also assume that our programs directly impact on business risk where we provide pre- and postevent mitigation services.

Metrics are embedded throughout the risk analysis process. Consider the opportunities for metrics, given the various components of risk assessment:

- *Assets* are measurable in a variety of ways; for example, current value, cost of replacement, cost of loss, and cost of downtime. Criticality ranking is a key element of the protection strategy that is discussed more fully in later sections.
- *Loss events* (historical and potential) have clear impact costs. A loss that was avoided is a direct benefit to the bottom line. Recoveries are an important event-follow-up metric.
- *Vulnerability* is measurable. Penetration delay times, table-top fault identification and analysis, electronic vulnerability testing, "black hat" operations, operational tests, and other means may be used to test various safeguards. (See section on Value Indicators later in this chapter.)

- *Likelihood* of a security-related event is more difficult to measure, but probabilities can be calculated. Insurance and risk management resources are often helpful. Some effort to postulate likelihood is essential to provide credibility to the stated risk. The presence of a not-addressed vulnerability is an obvious contributor to likelihood. Also, do not miss the fact that an attack elsewhere at another company on a similar asset type may represent a higher likelihood rating. Also, look at a more widely known (internally or externally, perhaps with a vendor or business "partner") vulnerability of a valued asset and consider factoring that into the higher likelihood potential.[2]
- *Options to mitigate vulnerabilities* are as measurable as the means to identify the exposures. If unacceptable downtimes for critical business processes were identified in a contingency planning test, alternate means of recovery would be imperative. Additional security measures to eliminate opportunities for intrusion are easily specified. Any protective option you select should have a corresponding measure of sought-after effectiveness. This need not be a complex mathematical formula but should indicate the estimated level of protective effectiveness based upon your selection of this safeguard.
- *Cost-benefit analysis* means weighing the cost of security improvements against the potential impact of loss, given an accepted measure of probability or likelihood of occurrence.

Any security executive not engaged in a continual process of risk assessment is failing in his or her central obligation to their employer. Risk is dynamic, constantly changing. Successful businesses are in constant states of change, presenting new risks or modifications to existing ones. Knowledge of risk imposes a duty (legal term! Knowledge imposes duty to take reasonable steps to mitigate) that involves answering key questions for management: How much risk? Could it happen here? Should we accept it, insure against it, or structure-specific countermeasures to mitigate it?

THOUGHT QUESTIONS

- The value equation: Can you identify a recent instance where a potential loss event was prevented by one or more safeguards in your security organization's toolkit?
- How are you cataloging these events to demonstrate security's contribution to the bottom line?
- How well did it work and what does this success suggest for further deployment of the protective strategy?

---

[2] The increasing reliance upon outsourced providers who are contracted to engage in services that provide access to very sensitive information and proprietary processes can significantly increase likelihood of loss exposure, especially where the company has failed to engage in a truly effective due diligence focused on the risks inherent in the services to be provided.

Risk rating or ranking[3]

From a security perspective, what is the riskiest facility, employee group, or business process in your company? Having performed a thorough risk analysis on a variety of critical facilities and business processes, how probable[4] are the selected risks and what are your priorities? Which ones present the most serious consequences? What should we do if the probability of loss is low but the potential impact is high? Which risks deserve more resources devoted to their mitigation than others?

There are at least two ways to view a risk-ranking scheme: as-is or mitigated. An as-is ranking takes the risk without consideration of application of any tailored countermeasures. The mitigated scheme assumes some measured level of protection afforded by the realistic capabilities of the countermeasures that you have applied. You are now in confidence territory. What if your level of "measured" protection was not the same as a well-prepared adversary? What if an insider was to disable the countermeasures or the security measure failed due to poor execution or any number of other failure potentials? From a pure risk-ranking perspective, you might do well to log as-is risk rankings and then really test your assumptions on the effectiveness of your protection strategy. This need not be a painful exercise. Risk rating is as simple as scoring risks as high, medium, or low; on a 1–5 scale; or as complex as applying algorithmic formulae. Try to develop some matrices that identify specific risks and align confidence levels to various safeguards. One example could be virus detection software with a 95% confidence level of detection and notification. Another example is preemployment background investigations with a confidence level of 80% that all derogatory information has been identified.

Another possible ranking scheme is shown in Figure 2.3. Using annual data, the CSO in this figure maintains an inventory of risky constituents using some key indicators believed to be relevant to a common sense discussion on the adequacy of local management attention, potential security intervention, and increased risk awareness. The overall scoring scheme is admittedly unscientific, but does enable the CSO to focus his or her planning and support a prioritization scheme. For obvious reasons, this is shared on a very limited basis but may be taken on a unit-by-unit basis to upper management where security's input is sought on business unit performance.

Work with your corporate risk manager (if your company has one) and internal audit[5] team to devise a methodology that makes sense for the types of strategies you

---

[3] This is not criticality ranking. Criticality focuses on the object of protection where risk ranking focuses on the threat and likelihood of that risk to the asset. Criticality should ultimately be translated into incident cost in financial terms wherever possible. This imposes a strong relationship with the asset owner.

[4] Probability of occurrence or loss is influenced by your prior event history, similar events elsewhere, environmental changes, loss frequency, trends, the presence of known vulnerabilities and the tested effectiveness of the security measures employed. It is not a mathematical absolute but a carefully considered assessment of likelihood.

[5] The Institute of Internal Auditors (IIA) can be very helpful in this area of risk assessment and elsewhere in the metrics and measures pursuit: www.theiia.org.

Alternate ranking scheme

Business unit	Headcount	Location risk	Internal incidents	Documented risk plan	Risky business processes	Risky hires	Terminations for cause	Info. security risk	Overall risk rank
Alpha	505	2	10	Yes	5	3	3	5	?
Beta	1,176	4	105	No	3	54	0	1	?
Gamma	203	3	4	Yes	2	0	1	2	?
Delta	1,459	5	213	No	4	21	17	2	?

FIGURE 2.3

An alternate ranking scheme can be to maintain an inventory of risky constituents. (For color version of this figure, the reader is referred to the online version of this book.)

are employing. Audit teams in particular, risk-rank business processes on a variety of measures and risk managers need to have the CSO's perspectives on operational risk.

What about maintaining a risk inventory?

An essential component of the learning process is the documentation of identified risks, the associated vulnerabilities, and the countermeasures that have proven to be effective in mitigating the risk. A risk inventory facilitates proactive security planning and a relative ranking process. An example of several items belonging to one category is shown in Figure 2.4.

Using caution with documentation of known risks

Keep in mind that acknowledged risk exposure, particularly where there are prior incidents, typically imposes a duty to prevent future occurrences. It would be advisable to engage your legal counsel (and risk manager) on the type of documentation and security classification needed for known risks within your company. In some cases, they may require the application of attorney–client privilege for certain types of risk documentation.

Risk mapping

Risk mapping refers to the process of plotting the dynamics of the risk incident landscape. A presentation model of risk dynamics (or risk profiling) may be found in Figure 2.5 below. More consequential incidents are at the top of the map and more frequent ones are to the right.

Cause analysis: internal misconduct incidents at Facility Alpha—June 1 through December 31, 2005

In this brief example (Figure 2.5), eight internal misconduct cases were plotted for the month and the six highlighted (incidents 1, 3, 4, 5, 6, and 8) all had inadequate

Risk category: Security program failure

Inadequate protection

- Negligent hiring and retention
- Illegal detention of citizen
- Failure to provide security where foreseeable crime is known
- Inadequate security equipment maintenance
- Inadequate system testing
- Inadequate security response
- Poor system design resulting in lack of user confidence/nuisance alarms
- Inadequate system monitoring and notification of alarm
- Violation of privacy
- Failure to detect/remove hazards
- Inadequate training of security personnel and other first responders
- Inadequate collection and protection of evidence
- Inadequate criminal investigation
- Failure to adequately protect rights of employees suspected of wrongdoing
- Failure to test and maintain fire detection and suppression equipment
- Inadequate testing of security response and evacuation plans

FIGURE 2.4

Sample risk inventory.

supervision and poor policy awareness as contributing causes of the infractions. Half were high severity, indicating a need to address these vulnerabilities quickly. When presented for a specific facility, manager or organization over time, this diagram can be very revealing and instructive. If this example proved to be common over multiple samples, it is obvious that the CSO would need to engage appropriate HR resources to review the content of supervisory training and performance

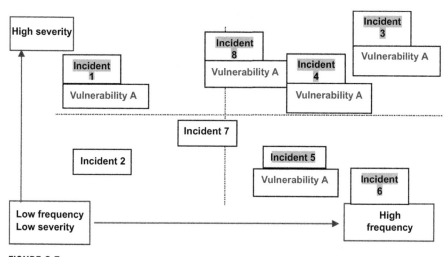

FIGURE 2.5

Sample risk map: Internal misconduct incidents at Facility Alpha—6/1 through December 31, 2005. (For color version of this figure, the reader is referred to the online version of this book.)

evaluation. A variety of risk profiles may be presented and analyzed in an Excel-based format. When contributing vulnerabilities or causes are noted in each cell, look for common denominators that can clearly demonstrate fundamental weaknesses in one control or another. A thorough examination of a case with an incident postmortem should yield contributing causes. There is a valuable story to be told to management and it is particularly useful in quarterly or annual presentations to display notable trends, their contributing causes, and suggestions for mitigation tactics. Work with your governance partners in this process.

TIPS FROM THE FIELD

Want to drill down on an emerging risk issue? Engage an audit colleague who is familiar with the targeted business process, along with the process owner(s), and find a white board. Break the process down and consider all the possibilities of how it could go wrong. Push the envelope on potential problems and solutions. You will build a supporter in that business unit and likely head off a developing area of risk.

Another approach to presenting risk information is to indicate movement and timing of incident types when various countermeasures were initiated. A similar—though single-issue—example is shown in Figure 2.6. During the 12-month period displayed in the figure, this company experienced a wave of laptop thefts. Incident postmortems clearly showed the failure of employees to secure their entrances, display their badge credentials and take custodial responsibility for company assets.

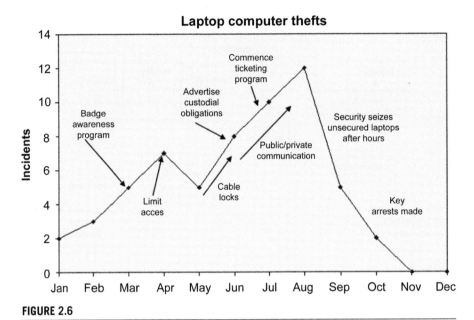

FIGURE 2.6

Graph of laptop computer thefts over a one-year period.

On the security side, increased sharing of similar incident data among downtown companies and police was used to identify several suspects. Security personnel conducted awareness briefings at staff meetings, introduced cable locks and initiated an aggressive inspection process resulting in unsecured laptops being seized and a "ticket" issued for failure to secure. The problem was virtually eliminated. But the more significant benefit was the fundamental change in employee behavior around taking responsibility for securing their space and partnering with security. It was reported that one senior executive went an interesting step further when he docked an employee's bonus after he lost a second laptop to poor custodial ownership.

THOUGHT QUESTIONS

- Select your three or four most risky incident categories, where you have 6–12 months of good data and investigative or analytical follow-up. Create a graph and plot each incident in terms of frequency and severity. Assign a scale to both criteria that makes the most sense for your organization. For example, frequency can be rated on a scale of 1–3, with 1 indicating one occurrence of the incident per month, 2 indicating two to three occurrences per month, and 3 indicating more than three occurrences per month. Severity might be rated on an escalating scale of the dollar amount of the loss incurred.
- Can you find any common denominators in the follow-up conclusions?
- How can you best display this data to influence corporate policy or attitudes?

Threat assessment

Did you include 9/11 in your threat inventory? How about a 100-year disaster event? Or did you consider that the CFO might be doing hard time for embezzlement? Risk assessment requires us to specify the source of the risk: the who or the what. Accident rates, weather-related disasters, exposure to fire given the level of protection we have in our facilities, critical system downtime data, redundancies, etc., all enable reasonably confident measures of probability. Tools such as crime forecasting data and maps by companies like CAP Index®[6] or other models enable estimates of exposure to various criminal and malevolent threats. Insider threats and other more sophisticated attacks require the analyst to specify a set of attack scenarios and then use them to assess the capabilities of the protection system to detect, deter, delay, and respond to each one. Prior audit or test findings on internal control deficiencies can give credibility to these subjective scenarios. Do not hesitate to use an incident elsewhere to demonstrate that it could happen to you, especially if it is in your business sector, or that it could happen given what you know about your company's vulnerabilities.

Figure 2.7 shows an example of an Excel bubble chart where each threat is sized from the analyst's estimate of organizational impact (severity) and displayed horizontally in terms of frequency.

THOUGHT QUESTIONS

Can you identify a threat *that you believe is credible* that you would hesitate to put forth to senior management?

Why hesitate?

What metrics or data could you assemble to provide a rational scenario for their consideration?

Vulnerability assessment

Drilling down within risk assessment will help you to find the real focus of a follow-up strategy: nailing down how exposed or vulnerable to compromise or loss a critical process or asset is. Vulnerabilities are flaws in protection that may be exploited by an adversary or a set of conditions that contribute to protection system failure. If there were to be a single compulsory rule for the asset custodian and the security team, it would be to have an ongoing program of identifying vulnerability of critical assets and business processes from specified threats. It is an interesting exercise to sit with a business process owner and ask, "If you wanted to [name the attack] this asset, how would you do it and avoid detection?" The actual incident postmortem is an ideal opportunity to identify vulnerability with one very notable exception: *it is too late.* Therefore, a theoretical postmortem allows you to identify vulnerabilities.

---

[6] For more information about CAP Index crime forecasting data, visit: http://www.capindex.com/.

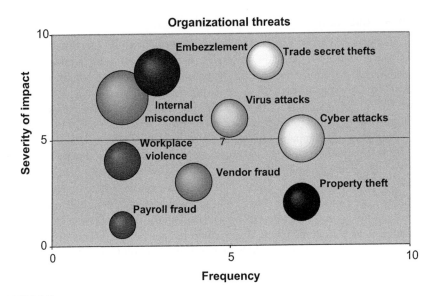

FIGURE 2.7

Impact of organizational threats.

Vulnerability is broad in scope and may be measured outright or opportunities for compromise can be estimated. Building weaknesses are exploitable and measurable. In most cases, access to the asset is measurable. Probability of detection is measurable. Protection systems can be disarmed, bypassed, or simply overlooked. People in key positions make mistakes, may be compromised, or have dishonest objectives of their own. If redundancies are not in place, you can measure the ability of employee response to preplanned events. You can apply covert and overt tests to measure efficacy of safeguards and, in some cases, you may want to employ trusted outside experts to test your security measures under carefully controlled conditions.

Several industry groups have developed and applied threat-specific and metric-centric vulnerability assessment tools to aid in consequence analysis, planning, and resource allocation, as well as to provide regulatory agencies with common baselines. This is particularly true around critical infrastructure protection. The following section summarizes an interesting vulnerability assessment process utilized by the Food and Drug Administration.[7] Check your assumptions about what could happen. Remember the adage: If things can go wrong, they likely will. "I should have known" is not the last thing you want to say as you collect your belongings from your desk.

---

[7] National Grain and Feed Association: CARVER Plus Shock Method for Food Sector Vulnerability Assessments, http://www.ngfa.org/pdfs/Carver_Shock_Primer.pdf. Accessed: 8/17/2005.

Overview of the CARVER+Shock method for food sector vulnerability assessments

The CARVER+Shock method is an offensive targeting prioritization tool—originally designed by the military—that has been adapted for use in the food sector. This tool can be used to assess the vulnerabilities within a system or infrastructure to an attack. It allows you to think like an attacker by identifying the most attractive targets for attack. By conducting such a vulnerability assessment and determining the most vulnerable points in your infrastructure, you can then focus your resources on protecting your most vulnerable points.

CARVER is an acronym for the following six attributes used to evaluate the attractiveness of a target for attack:

- Criticality: Measure of public health and economic impacts of an attack.
- Accessibility: Ability to physically access and egress from the target.
- Recuperability: Ability of the system to recover from an attack.
- Vulnerability: Ease of accomplishing an attack.
- Effect: Amount of direct loss from an attack as measured by loss in production.
- Recognizability: Ease of identifying the target.

In addition, the modified CARVER tool evaluates a seventh attribute: the combined health, economic, and psychological impacts of an attack, or the Shock attributes of a target. The attractiveness of a target can then be ranked on a scale from one to ten on the basis of scales that have been developed for each of the seven attributes. Conditions that are associated with lower attractiveness (or lower vulnerability) are assigned lower values (e.g., 1 or 2), whereas conditions associated with higher attractiveness as a target (or higher vulnerability) are assigned higher values (e.g., 9 or 10). Evaluating or scoring the various elements of the food sector infrastructure of interest for each of the CARVER+Shock attributes can help identify where within that infrastructure, an attack is most likely to occur. Federal agencies, such as the Food Safety and Inspection Service and the Food and Drug Administration, have used this method to evaluate the potential vulnerabilities of farm-to-table supply chains of various food commodities. The method can also be used to assess the potential vulnerabilities of individual facilities or processes.

Cost-effectiveness analysis

What tools, methods, techniques, or countermeasures are best qualified to achieve the necessary security enhancements identified in the risk analysis? Only those enhancements that are projected to be the most effective at the lowest possible costs are selected for final consideration. Costs may be one-time or continuing and benefits are typically realized over time via a projected payback period. Discipline is required here to adequately specify the costs associated with the most credible loss probabilities and the costs of your alternative protection tactics.[8] It is fairly straightforward

---

[8] See the ASIS International *General Security Risk Assessment Guideline* for a comprehensive treatment of probability estimation. Visit ASIS International at www.asisonline.org/.

to nail down the most evident costs that come from new policies, personnel assignments, and equipment purchases. But remember the opening exercise in Chapter 1 about calculating the cost of security. Pay attention to the peripheral or secondary costs that accrue with the implementation of a new security program.

Leading indicators

Leading indicators signal future risk or security-related events. They are measurable factors that change before the risk starts to follow a particular pattern or trend. A security example might be an increase in derogatory background investigation statistics for a certain area or type of employee applicant. If such a person were hired, it might be predictive of potential future internal misconduct depending upon the nature of behavioral information revealed in the background case. Another example is the increase in unaddressed nuisance or false intrusion alarms as predictive of a successful intrusion (Figure 2.8).

THOUGHT QUESTIONS

- Can you identify sloppy employee security practices around information security or other programs that represent leading indicators?
- For example, can you demonstrate that poor patch administration has resulted in damaging virus attacks or that failure to label or secure proprietary information has led to loss of vital data?
- How would you approach the business unit executive with this information to gain attitude adjustment? What would your next step be if you failed to gain the requisite compliance?

Lagging indicators

A lagging indicator is one that follows an event. Lagging indicators confirm long-term trends, but do not predict them. An increase in successful intrusion is a lagging indicator following the nuisance alarm example noted in Figure 2.8. Another might be the number of internal incidents where failure in supervisory oversight is cited as a causal factor.

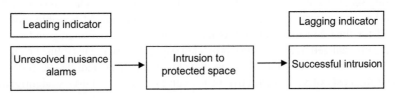

FIGURE 2.8

Leading and lagging indicators.

Value indicators

Value indicators typically provide information on what or how much the security function(s) are contributing to enterprise health and profitability. For example, an investigative organization that costs $500,000 annually but recovers $1,000,000 has a measurably positive ROI. Trickier measures are around issues that are less concrete, like prevention of an incident or the degree to which a proactive business conduct program contributes to reduced incidents of internal crime or misconduct. An interesting exercise is to work with your human resources department to determine the fiscal cost of a dishonest employee who might have been caught by an effective background vetting process or a more aware and engaged supervisor. The cost is significant when you tally the both the time and cost of the dishonest employee's life cycle. Consider these steps generally involved in the "bad" employee cycle:

Steps in the "bad employee" cycle

1. Loss of effective performance of the incumbent and supervisory trust during notification of investigation and relief from duty resulting from investigation.
2. Time to resolution of investigation ending in approved termination.
3. Time to post and initiate recruitment process.
4. Replacement candidate review and selection.
5. Initial hire time including selectee's release from current employment.
6. Downtime from hire date to reasonably full performance.
7. The potential (actual or reputational) damage caused by the incident attributable to him/her if the incident becomes public knowledge.
8. The cost of the investigation, termination, or prosecution.
9. The cost of staffing and backfilling (including external headhunter posthire costs) for the now vacant position.
10. The cost of orientation and training the new employee.
11. The potential fallout within the affected business unit.
12. Assuming the matter has been contained, the potential cost of lost business if the knowledgeable, well-positioned, and now terminated former employee goes to work for the competition with no clue on their part that they have hired a bad guy. Why? Because they never ask what happened with this employee (and your HR department would not have told them even if they asked).

TIPS FROM THE FIELD

Working with your human resource department, use these steps and any others that may apply to your organization's response to the termination and backfilling of a position and assign a cost to each. This number makes a powerful statement on the cost of a "bad" employee and the obligation of management to set the tone and be proactive in oversight.

Good reporting and tracking provides valuable indicators of recurring incidents, and their frequency increases predictability. From a value perspective, where responsive security measures are applied and proven effective, we may say that we have prevented the costs associated with incident response and recovery and demonstrated an ROI. Simple examples are found around successful accident prevention programs and installation of effective virus protection software after frequent incidents resulting in downtime of critical systems.

THOUGHT QUESTIONS

- You have just been called into a meeting of the new cost management committee and asked what two examples you would offer to demonstrate how security is contributing to making the company more cost competitive and what you would eliminate if you were asked to reduce your expense by 50%.
- What would you tell them about the consequences of your choices to address the 50% reduction?
- What would be your answer to "Thanks, but we will accept the risk?"

Appendix 1 has more examples of measures and metrics. There are a significant number of metrics that may be utilized as indicators of corporate security's value. You will note that some are framed positively and others in negative terms. The choice of phrasing is yours depending upon how you seek to characterize that metric.

Criticality ranking

Criticality ranking is a vital part of administering a proactive security risk management program. It provides a large metric-based inventory of assets and essential resources. It asks the question: "Given threats and vulnerabilities to specific assets or business processes, what is unacceptable to the corporation? What is our tolerance for risk in this instance?" Further, how "unacceptable" are these threats? What and how much resource should we devote to reducing this exposure to an acceptable level?" This qualitative and quantitative ranking process is as broad and deep as the number of processes involved in achieving the goals of the business.

Where an enterprise depends upon a consumer perception of honesty, integrity, safety, or other measurable expectation, this exercise is a cornerstone of the protection and recovery strategy. Which assets deserve the most protection at what response times? How severe will loss of process functionality or denial of the asset be? The criticality ranking of a process or resource is a core assessment in business continuity planning. The amount of time that we can maintain a critical operation without the asset in question is a metric.[9] If zero downtime is the verifiable conclusion for that metric, then a financial consequence of loss can be estimated, as are calculations for

---

[9] For example: AAA = immediate recovery. No downtime allowed. Requires implementing an in-place, fully equipped and staffed alternate site. AA = up to 4 h to recover, A = same day recovery, B = up to 24 h recovery, C = 24–72 h recovery, D = 72 h or greater recovery.

recovery timelines and cost of redundancy or backup resources. On some measurable scale, what are the actual financial, reputational, or operational consequences of disruption? What is the loss or damage to each asset, person, or process deemed essential to delivery of the core business? The CSO has a unique perspective on understanding which assets, resources, or processes are truly essential to the health and integrity of the corporation's operations. This focus provides defensible prioritization and a fundamental rationale for the protection strategy.

THOUGHT QUESTIONS

- If you had only the resources to protect the three most critical business resources in your company, what would they be and why?
- What is your two to three sentence summary protection strategy for each one?
- What would your CEO say about your selection and the strategies you have identified?

Confidence and influence indicators

Unlike some regulated industries, most businesses' security cannot be implemented by edict. Many business executives will balk at security policies they see as unnecessary cost drivers or productivity constraints. Remember: *Effective CSOs work in an environment of influence.*

Confidence or influence indicators are particularly important in the assessment of corporate security relationships and they are measurable. The quality of the business relationships established by security executives and their services go directly to the ability of the security functions to provide real value to the business operations they are organized to serve. What is the difference between a business unit that responds to a security recommendation and avoids an incident and the business unit that disrespects or dismisses the source and content and the result is eventual loss or other consequences? The difference will likely show up as a cost that is measurable. An annual client satisfaction survey (which all security organizations should conduct) can provide a wealth of feedback on the effectiveness of security's messages, identify the soft spots in security awareness, and focus the CSO on the performance of the department and its people. It is also an example of a leading indicator. It is strongly recommended that you poll a sample that includes both prior customers of security's services and others in the service population. Responses should be conducted to provide respondent anonymity where desired but enable identification of the business unit where the respondent works in order to accommodate potential corrective actions.

An important aspect of confidence measures is the notion of CSO or program influence. "How do I measure my ability to influence senior management and the culture and practices of this organization?" The Security Program Legitimacy Index (SPLI) outlined in Table 2.2 represents one example of a CSO's set of confidence or influence measures.

Table 2.2 Security Program Legitimacy Index

SPLI

Rate 1 (low) to 5 (high) your confidence that the statement applies in your organization.

Operational effectiveness. There is clear evidence that security programs work to protect the enterprise and its people and create respect and support for those programs and security's leadership.

The CSO has unhindered access to the top. The boss knows who you are and answers the phone when you call.

Corporate security can influence the strategic direction of the business. Security has to be an enabler of business success and competitiveness. If you make it less risky to do business, you are contributing to the bottom line in real numbers and giving the business an edge.

Corporate security is an acknowledged stakeholder in the corporate risk management program. The CSO has a well-placed chair at the risk management and corporate governance table.

When security issues are escalated, there are no surprises. This is another view of access but keyed to bypassing the guy who says "do not tell the boss." Delivering bad news goes with the job.

Management connects security's program with value delivered. Business leadership connects a value (competitive, risk avoidance, personal safety, etc.) to security's programs and operations.

Senior management responds appropriately to security's proposals. The CSO knows how to sell the program and top management listens. This does not mean unquestioned or 100% acceptance.

Senior management exhibits clear support of security policy. The CSO has articulated a risk-responsive set of high-level policy statements that top management understands and supports with resources and reinforcement.

Security has sufficient resources to accomplish the protection mission. Your programs are deemed worth the price. Sufficient to deliver on the policies, not excessive or gold plated.

Security's programs have a positive impact on the ethical hygiene of the firm. Security's programs and leadership reinforce a culture of doing the right thing and deliver key services in support of the system of internal controls. Moreover, customers have high confidence in security's attention to their concerns and in the integrity of its people and operations.

The CSO exercises exclusive ownership of the firm's security program. This envisions all security services under one executive, the CSO, but may also be served by the CSO chairing a security committee comprised of all related services and other members of the governance infrastructure.

Security's customer base exhibits broad knowledge of security program components and risk awareness. A key indicator that the CSO knows how to reach the people and influence behavior and individual responsibility. Security has successfully sold the notion that the maintenance of security is a shared responsibility with employees and business management.

The SPLI is another way to look at confidence in the security function and particularly the CSO's measure of legitimacy or clout with senior management. Factors may be selectively applied or other measures more appropriate to the reader's environment may be substituted. The purpose of the exercise is to identify several measurable qualities, competencies, performance evaluation criteria, organizational capabilities, or other empirical indicators of security's influence and ability to provide risk management leadership across the enterprise. You are to score each item from 1 (low confidence) to 5 (highest confidence) on whether that statement applies to the CSO and the security program. Sixty is the highest possible score, but that is not as relevant as deciding which ones really do apply in your organization and, given an honest answer to each, what steps you would propose taking to remedy any shortcomings if you believe the factor applies. You may decide that only a few apply. What are your answers?

Each of the statements in the SPLI deserves thoughtful, honest consideration. Your list should be verified by knowledgeable and objective peers and superiors. You may decide that one or more do not apply but try to substitute ones that do fit a model that is accommodated in your corporate culture. If you feel good about the results, *do not become overconfident*. Things can change overnight.

Security standards (a.k.a. guidelines)

Although the climate is shifting, those who still argue that security is not yet a profession often hang their hat on the absence of a code of practice and body of standards within its ranks. This is another reflection of the lack of an established model of corporate security. The debate on security standards often turns on the concern that once established they will be adopted by insurance carriers and legislative bodies and drive up the cost of doing business as well as liability exposure. This is certainly true in the life-safety arena. However, security standards have been developed by a number of well-established U.S. and international trade and professional societies. The inventory is extensive within the life-safety, information security, contingency planning, physical security technology, and government security realms and provides a variety of measurable indicators. The subject matter of these standards is diverse and may not be applicable to your environment but should provide opportunities for customization. Security and safety-related standards typically involve measurement processes and resulting metrics. Consider the following statements from the National Fire Protection Association (NFPA) 1600 Standard on Disaster/Emergency Management and Business Continuity Programs[10]:

- **5.3.1** The entity shall identify hazards, the likelihood of their occurrence, and the vulnerability of people, property, the environment, and the entity itself to those hazards.

---

[10] National Fire Protection Association, NFPA 1600, Standard on Disaster/Emergency Management and Business Continuity Programs (Quincy, MA: National Fire Protection Association, 2004).

- The explanatory material interprets this statement in part as follows:

   "A.5.3.3 The impact analysis is a broad description and quantification of a potential event that can impact an entity. This analysis should give a clear idea of what hazards are most likely to occur; what entity facilities, functions, or services are affected based on their vulnerability to that hazard; what actions will most effectively protect them; and the potential impact on the entity in quantifiable terms."

"Quantifiable" means just what it says. You are to demonstrate in verifiable metric terms the degree of likelihood, vulnerability, and consequences of multiple man-made, accidental, and natural disaster events. Insurance carriers and risk managers base their positions on a quantifiable foundation. (Note, since 9/11, regulatory standards in the security field are abandoning the term "should" in favor of "must.")

Every corporate/information security organization should develop a set of core security policies supported by measurable standards where appropriate.[11] But exercise caution. Where developed internally by a service organization like security, the term "standard" often causes extreme discomfort with line business management as it is seen as driving cost and centralized control. ASIS International and other organizations have understood the term "guidelines" tends to be more palatable to management, even if the language remains largely the same. Security executives need to be particularly concerned where individual organizational units within the corporate family seek to develop their own security standards. This is particularly true for information security, where individual business units may have the ability to deploy their uniquely selected hardware and software components that will ultimately operate on the corporate network.

The development of security standards should be approached with a collaborative interdepartmental initiative that relies heavily on risk assessment data. Where a pattern of measurable risk across multiple sites can be established, the rationale for an industry-accepted set of safeguards (or standards) is far more supportable. You may also find support within specific regulatory regimes that apply to the organization but, at the end of the day, the culture will define the approach to establishing a framework that will support the notions of "must do" and "should do." Remember that "must do" imposes cost and compliance will frequently require a process of incremental or stepped improvement.

THOUGHT QUESTIONS

- If there were only one standard you could implement in your organization that in your judgment would make a measurable improvement in the security of your company, what would it be, and why would compliance have the result you would anticipate?
- How would you measure success?
- How would you advertise the results to leverage even greater improvements?

---

[11] Revisit "The CSO's Context for Metrics" section in Chapter 1. Keep the total framework for policies in mind and make sure you understand how policies and standards are accepted and framed in your organization.

Task analysis and work breakdown structures

If you are concerned about the cost and efficiency of a security process, you will invariably engage in task analysis. Task analysis involves breaking the process down into its most definable and measurable elements. It is typically a shock when a disciplined task or process analysis is applied to security practices because it is so rarely done. This type of analysis is routinely accomplished in incredible detail in manufacturing, construction, system engineering, and other technical fields. What you think is a relatively straightforward set of defined tasks becomes a revealing set of interconnected steps, all of which may be risk-analyzed, person-hour-timed, and cost-estimated. For example, consider processing a simple call to the security control center that an employee may be having a heart attack, as shown in Table 2.3.

A high-level work breakdown structure for a security program is included in Appendix 2. It is important to take each element and carefully evaluate how that item further links to interrelated subtasks that are capable of reliable time and cost estimating.

Project cost estimating

Project cost estimating is an example of applying task analysis to a specific project. New requirements are increasingly placed on the CSO's plate and the work has to be broken down into its distinct parts to consider what needs to be done and how much

Table 2.3 Steps for a Security Control Center Call

Steps	Analysis
Receive call informing employee emergency	How long to answer?
Obtain key information on location and nature of illness	How complete and in what time to gather essential information for timely dispatch?
Determine closest security officer (SO) with requisite training to aid victim	How long to identify correct SO? How long will it take to arrive? Will 911 be faster? Is the training of SOs adequate?
Dispatch SO to location	How long from dispatch to arrival at scene?
Notify 911 and provide essential information	Time elapsed since call receipt? How long will emergency medical services (EMS) take to arrive?
Inform supervisor	Supervisory approval of action?
Log essential data	Is logged data complete?
Receive radio message SO has arrived	Time elapsed?
Receive message SO has stabilized victim	Adequacy of aid? Lessons learned? Later feedback from victim on service?
Receive message EMS has arrived and is transporting victim to hospital	Time elapsed from notification to arrival? Adequacy of response at scene?

each element will cost. You cannot do the cost trade-offs and benefit analysis until you have fairly accurately estimated the going cost. Examples include:

1. Your company has a new CEO and a reconstituted board of directors, all of whom are very concerned about ethics. You have concluded that no real effort has been made to address the Corporate Sentencing Guidelines and now Counsel has asked you to address the 2010 amendments to include a cost estimate to demonstrate a good faith effort at compliance. (See Table 2.4, originally developed for *The Cost of Compliance* by the Security Executive Council.)

2. Your global physical access control/alarm management system is outdated. You have to prepare a cost estimate that is expected to run into the millions of dollars. It would be foolish to rely on a vendor to give you the estimate with all the elements of cost when you cannot afford to hire a consultant to do the planning and estimating. A large project like this might well have a work breakdown structure of several hundred items, each with an associated cost. Your purchasing department and/or facilities staff will be of assistance here but they may have little or no experience with the strategy and equipment involved. Do not give up on the project, though. Find a colleague who has recently completed a project of this type and learn from that experience.

3. General Counsel has just notified you that you have to launch a major internal investigation that will hopefully yield recovery costs. It will involve scores of interviews and related investigative tasks in several countries and you need to hire consultants or redirect scarce internal resources. This project will likely be very costly and you need to provide Counsel an estimate of what to expect.

4. Your company has just lost a critical facility to natural disaster and you now realize that local management has failed to backup important files and preposition essential resources at an alternate site. What is it going to cost the company to recover from this disaster and how long will it take?

There are as many examples as there are potential needs to devote resources to achieving some specific objective. Task analysis and project cost estimating are exercises in planning, budgeting, and scheduling. Measures and metrics are used throughout the steps involved.

Baseline performance metrics

Every security function will have embedded performance metrics and related measures. Appendix 1 in this volume provides a comprehensive listing of metrics but primarily serves to form a basis for the reader to develop and add those most appropriate to their operations and the business drivers of the organization(s) they serve. A few examples follow in Figures 2.9, 2.10, and 2.11.

Response times for first responders, both within the security organization as well as public emergency services, represent critical expectations, particularly where life-safety issues are involved. Consider the results shown in Figure 2.9. The corporation

Table 2.4 Cost Estimate for 2005 Revisions to the U.S. Sentencing Commission Guidelines for Organizations

Cost Estimate for 2005 Revisions to the U.S. Sentencing Commission Guidelines for Organizations (Assume a large cap company with $12.5 billion in revenues and 30,000 employees)	
Full-time, senior management individual reporting to the board of directors (or a committee of the board) with day-to-day responsibility for compliance and ethics program ("an effective program to prevent and detect violation of law"). Median compensation for ethics officers at $225,000 base and this deemed more senior.	• Salary and bonus: $400,000+38% benefits=$552,000
Adequate resources and authority for the job: Full-time administrative assistant ($55,000+38%=$75,900+1 professional-level position @ $125,000×38%=$172,500). An additional 2 FTEs at similar level to latter drawn upon over course of year.	• Full-time staff: $248,400 • Part-time staff resources: $345,000
Employment-related background checks @ $125.00 ea.×1000 annually for model purposes.	• Background investigations: $125,000 • Administration within Corporate Security—1 Admin. Asst. @ same as above: $75,900
Internal investigations to determine whether an individual has engaged in "other conduct inconsistent with an effective program." Estimate 100 internal misconduct/criminal investigations annually by corporate security @ average of 240h each=24,000h @ consolidated hourly rate of $50.00/h. (If substituting internal investigations conducted by external consultants engaged by General Counsel, assume 24,000h @ $200.00/h=$2,400,000. Not utilized in this example.)	• Internal investigations conducted by Corporate Investigations: $1,200,000
"Appropriate incentives to perform in accordance with the compliance and ethics program" are deemed to be bonuses tied to revised annual performance review processes. For purposes of this example assume an average of $5000×200 employees annually.	• Incentive recognition: $1,000,000

Continued

Table 2.4 Cost Estimate for 2005 Revisions to the U.S. Sentencing Commission Guidelines for Organizations—cont'd

Cost Estimate for 2005 Revisions to the U.S. Sentencing Commission Guidelines for Organizations (Assume a large cap company with $12.5 billion in revenues and 30,000 employees)	
Mandatory compliance training: Assume program will be developed and administered internally. Training program development & administration within Human Resources—2080h @ $50/h=$104,000, Contractor support @ $75,000, 1000h of training the trainers @ $50/h=$50,000, training sessions attended by 1000 employees and board members and 200 external vendor agents for 2h each at fully loaded average of $100/h=$240,000.	• Compliance training: $469,000
Development of "auditing and monitoring systems to detect criminal conduct." Several external computer based models are being evaluated. Guidance is clear that the corporation must be able to demonstrate that it employed and acted upon documented monitoring systems. (The cost of the detection system for conduct should be in the compliance unit cost center. The cost for auditing the businesses, to see they meet compliance requirements, is quite different and goes to total overhead.) For purposes of example, assume Internal Audit/Corporate Security develop an Integrity Assessment model used in targeted audits of risk-prone business units—240h @ $50/h=$12,000.	• Modifications to Audit process: $12,000
"Periodic evaluation of the effectiveness of the program." Assume Board requires an annual assessment by the firm's external auditors.	• Compliance program evaluation: $250,000
Review and readvertise the Employee Confidential Line for reporting suspected criminal conduct and wrongdoing. Review component included in the external review above.	• Readvertise hotline: $12,000
Mandatory risk assessment process to "periodically assess the risk of criminal conduct and shall take appropriate steps to design, implement, or modify each requirement to reduce the risk of criminal conduct identified through this process." Assume Board will require an external assessment by a qualified contractor other than the external auditors to preserve independence.	• Contracted risk analysis: $250,000

Table 2.4 Cost Estimate for 2005 Revisions to the U.S. Sentencing Commission Guidelines for Organizations—cont'd

Cost Estimate for 2005 Revisions to the U.S. Sentencing Commission Guidelines for Organizations (Assume a large cap company with $12.5 billion in revenues and 30,000 employees)	
Estimated Total Cost of Compliance	$4,538,900
Options for recovery of cost via accounting pass-through to business units must be evaluated on a case-by-case basis. It is feasible that some measure of costs of the core Compliance Office or other activities noted above may be classified as an element of internal controls and cost-of-business but this has to be assessed individually.	
A modified version of this table originally appeared in The Cost of Compliance *developed by the Security Executive Council*	

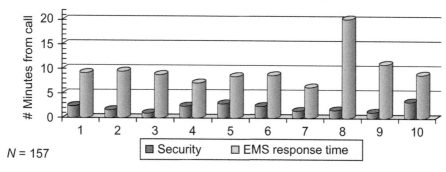

FIGURE 2.9

Average medical response time by city, 2013. In this example, the cities in which the example corporation has locations with security personnel are assigned a number and charted on the X-axis. (For color version of this figure, the reader is referred to the online version of this book.)

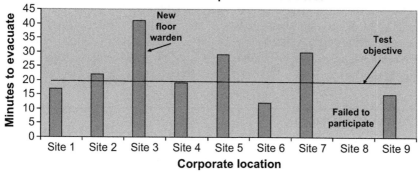

FIGURE 2.10

Evacuation drill test times.

in this example has a high quality proprietary security operations division and has invested in significant first responder training. Moreover, it has imposed a 3- to 5-min response objective on itself for high priority calls for service. It is not surprising that lives have been saved in medical emergencies here, and these metrics are a dramatic demonstration of that performance and value.

Prior to 9/11, it was a periodic test of wills and a near fatal exercise for the CSO to convince business units that evacuation drills were an essential part of doing business. This is now an expectation of any and every company. (Although, as time passes the "cannot be bothered" syndrome resettles in the office.) In Figure 2.10, Company ABC has compared nine *comparable* facilities for their respective test results and the CSO intends to include this slide in the next briefing for the risk management committee. These drills were well advertised and are a requirement of their insurance carrier's policy.

THOUGHT QUESTIONS

- What time factors are critical within your security environment?
- What metrics do you employ to track this critical area of performance?
- Who are the recipients of your assessment(s) and how do they react to your reporting? Have you adequately integrated them into the assessment process?

Timelines to recover from business interruption are essential measures that drive business continuity planning. Anticipated time to respond to cyber and physical intrusion alarms should be part of a proactive resource deployment strategy. Process completion or cycle times are performance measures that clients impose or that are incorporated into SLAs. Examples are human resources and the hiring business unit cycle time for a background investigation result or an important outsourcing decision awaiting a clean bill of health from a due diligence examination.

Figure 2.11 shows two simple security cost examples maintained monthly on an Excel spreadsheet. These leading indicators (trend line, solid; actual, hatched) may be tracked to alert to unfavorable trends and report quarterly on security's efforts to manage cost. Security cost per square foot of occupied space (a notable indicator in space cost) and per employee continues positive downward trends. There is a good value story to be told here.

TIPS FROM THE FIELD

Examine your historical security program costs over the past five years vs some examples in your business that would enable proportionate comparison. Security cost vs. gross or net revenues, etc. See Appendix 5 for additional examples.

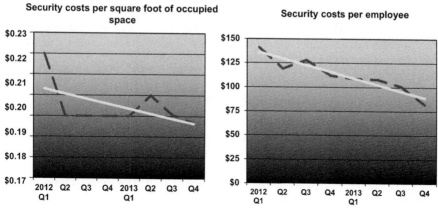

FIGURE 2.11

Monthly security costs.

There are many baseline performance measures for various security functions. Below are some representative examples, some of which may be a basic expectation of management.

- Investigation results like case closure with successful prosecution and full recovery.
- Malicious code prevention and timely securing of vital data and process after a virus or other cyber attack.
- Reduced cycle times with correspondingly lower costs for background investigations, due diligence examinations, and other process-specific investigative procedures.
- Definitive response to an environmental alarm in a lights-out data center.
- Software patch administration has become a critical security process with indices like number of compliant vs noncompliant servers.
- Percentage of critical business processes in each business unit with up-to-date and tested plans.

Can you demonstrate you are doing more with less, such as reduced cost with increased volumes over a specific time period? Or protecting more space and people with less protective service employees than the competition? It is essential to identify and track key cost indicators appropriate to the security mission. Examples might be quarterly security cost per employee, per square foot, repetitive process costs, recoveries vs net losses in check frauds, etc. Public sector performance metrics will tend to focus on efficiency (process cycle times, paperwork reduction, case management, response times, cost reductions, etc.) and mission effectiveness (SWOT analysis—strengths, weaknesses, opportunities, threats; customer satisfaction; clearance rates; successful prosecutions; reduced recidivism rates; etc.).

The type of operations and the focus of protection will drive sets of performance metrics that should be applied and reported. They become expectations of management and provide substance for departmental and individual performance measurement. Several examples are found throughout Appendix 1.

Estimated incident costing and consequence analysis

Estimated incident costing and consequence analysis is similar to criticality ranking but more tuned to gaining an understanding of the total financial impact of various incident scenarios. Various types of risks can be inventoried with costs and potential consequences estimated in cooperation with the business process owners. The CFO and internal audit can be of assistance as well. The simplest form of risk assessment lists the likely risks and vulnerabilities confronting the business with a 1 (low) to 5 (high) consequence ranking. An incident likelihood multiplier may be added to discount or emphasize the risk presented by the findings. Where a business process is vitally dependent on a specific platform, application, supplier, or other resource, you can pretty much guarantee that they know the consequences of loss. These people worry about time to recover (TtR) and single points of failure and are likely to have built redundancies into their strategy. Depending on the quality and level of interaction between security and client business units, security practitioners should take note of the fact that many business units fail to consider criminal and manmade threats in their analyses of potential business interruption events.

The ASIS *General Security Risk Assessment Guideline*[12] offers a number of means of calculating cost of loss. One formula they offer is based on a worst-case scenario in which each security loss risk is analyzed for the possible maximum loss where the risk event to occur once. The formula—or equation—is as follows:

$$K = (Cp + Ct + Cr + Ci) - I$$

where:

K=criticality, total cost of loss;
Cp=cost of permanent replacement;
Ct=cost of temporary substitute;
Cr=total related costs;
Ci=lost income cost; and
I=available insurance or indemnity.

The corporate finance or risk management organization may provide specific guidance on an accepted means of presenting loss and other financial consequence estimates. The Risk Management Society and the Insurance Information Institute (III) are useful sources for risk and loss measures and statistics.

---

[12]ASIS International, *General Security Risk Assessment Guideline* (Alexandria, VA: ASIS International, 2003).

When performing a risk-benefit calculation, it is often helpful to factor in the annualized loss expectancy (ALE) of an asset. This is the expected loss of value (monetary) of any given asset over the course of the fiscal year. Albion Research, Ltd, a Canada-based risk management consultancy, discusses the concept of ALE at length on their website.[13]

The business unit security scorecard

Depending on how the CSO manages the assessment process (see Table 2.5 for an example), the scorecard method can be a very effective means of obtaining improvement in business unit conformance with security policy and guidance. If the assessment process is badly managed it may just result in a ticket to the unemployment line for the security executive. The scorecard process must be pre-sold with senior management, and depending on the type of issues covered and potential vulnerability implications, the application of privilege in cooperation with general counsel or under the aegis of internal audit work papers should be considered.

Note the use of symbols in Table 2.5 to accent positives and highlight deficiencies in a simple format. In this example, the business unit is seriously deficient in several aspects of control oversight (marked with a ► symbol). They also are exposed through risky oversight by the human resources department. Without satisfactory corrective action, a referral to internal audit or escalation to senior management would be the likely protocol. Areas of positive action (contingency plan status, due diligence follow-up) are marked with a ♦ symbol. Areas that fall between the two, those that require cautious watching, are left unmarked. You can use any method to mark these areas (shading, colors, symbols) in order to highlight successes and areas that need improvement. It may be easiest to highlight deficient areas in red, areas that need cautious watching in yellow, and areas of positive action in green. Where this or similar annual reviews have been appropriately established and conducted, the results have also found their way into the business unit manager's bonus reviews—an outcome guaranteed to legitimize the process and gain compliance on a far more proactive basis.

The situation in Table 2.5 underscores the need for the CSO to decide how the scorecard process will be conducted. A more collegial, business-partner-to-business-partner approach may be a positive way to gain support, one customer at a time. A hard-nosed CEO and board may expect the CSO to do equally hard-nosed "security audits" and let the chips fall where they may. Appendix 1 contains examples that may be used on a scorecard depending on your organizational needs and opportunities. As to phrasing, you can decide how to best build a model that is appropriate to your corporate culture.

---

[13] Albion Research, "Annualized Risk Expectancy (Definition)," accessed September 13, 2013, http://www.riskythinking.com/glossary/annualized_loss_expectancy.php.

Table 2.5 Sample Business Unit Scorecard

Business Unit Assessment: Accountable Manager, Alan Jones	
Summary: Company ABC has had a difficult year with revenue shortfalls that have required Mr. Jones to focus heavily on reducing cost and improving market penetration rather than the infrastructure improvements we agreed were appropriate at our last security review. However, the risk implications of the annual review results noted below could have serious impacts across the company given ABC's network connections and ownership of significant proprietary information that may be at risk. Actions taken: • Referral to Internal Audit for follow-up on information security vulnerabilities is recommended. • Meeting scheduled with CEO to support ABC's prior commitments and provide context for enterprise risk. • Open access to perimeter doors removed and card access only imposed. • Security awareness program initiated in key areas. • Corporate security will devote X resources to supporting risk mitigation activities based on mutually developed plan. • ABC Information Security Officer replaced with known resource. • HR SVP Smith advised of inadequate vetting by subordinate unit; agrees to retraining and monitoring. Agrees to look into follow-up actions on internal cases and get back to CSO with resolution.	
Backgrounds of candidate pool past year	► 20% serious derogatory rate indicates poor HR applicant vetting
Business unit action on background investigations	► 75% hire rate on serious BI issues
Contingency plan status	♦ Successful walk-through and annual test. Good alternate site plan
Due diligence follow-up	♦ All outsource relationships reported as having significant risk concerns have been terminated
Information security risk assessment status	► +90 days behind schedule
Applications in compliance with password policy	► 50% compliant + shared passwords
Protection of company-sensitive materials	► Frequent violations noted: Internet abuse, lost laptops, failure to store proprietary information as required
Timeliness of software patching	Some deficiencies noted in review. Concern if this inaction spreads to more critical applications
Follow-up to internal investigations Willingness to address vulnerabilities noted in internal incident postmortems	Failure to apply agreed-upon employee sanctions in 3 of 8 cases

The point of the process is to better align with business, celebrate good security practices, and obtain voluntary behavior modification and improvement where deficiencies are confirmed. The sharp stick in the eye of escalation to higher authority will likely be more effective after attempting to influence the scorecard recipient on the risk exposure.[14]

THOUGHT QUESTIONS

- What are the dangers associated with the scorecard process within your organization, and what could you do to minimize these potential problems in customer relations?
- What issues would you choose to measure and report to your two most challenging constituents? What about your two most supportive constituents? How are they different and why?
- If your boss were preparing a scorecard on the security organization, what would you expect to see in the ► and ♦ areas? Why? What would be your plan using the strengths from the ♦ areas to address the concerns in the others? How would you approach areas that fall between the two—areas that require cautious watching?

Diagnostic measures[15]

Drivers are all familiar with the highway sign "Dangerous Curve Ahead Reduce Speed." Many of the measures discussed here may be applied as a way to provide the CSO and key constituents with caution signals. They become the earliest prompts for more in-depth analysis of trend dynamics. A word of caution, though: Be sure you are looking at the root causes, not just the symptoms. The following are examples of diagnostic measures a CSO might use.

- Increased frequency and/or severity of accident, crime, or policy infraction rates.
- Reduced mean time between failures on critical equipment with increased downtime.
- Increased or more serious derogatory background investigation rates in specific hiring populations.
- Excessive passwords for access to different "secure" applications resulting in sloppy security practices like sharing and visible posting.
- Increasing process cycle times, out-of-normal response times to calls for service.
- Outsourcing sensitive business processes without requisite due diligence and vendor risk analysis or contractual safeguards.
- Increased misconduct or workplace violence incidents in specific facilities or departments.

---

[14] Also see the risk-ranking scheme earlier in this chapter.

[15] For an excellent discussion on this and related issues relevant to measuring business controls, see Robert Simons, "Control in an Age of Empowerment," *Harvard Business Review* (March 01, 1995).

- Elimination or reduced testing of building evacuation plans with consequent confusion and injury in real incidents.
- Degradation of timely software patch application or increased virus activity in specific client groups.

Appendix 3 contains several examples of diagnostic indicators. The following section discusses one of the more important topical areas for monitoring.

THOUGHT QUESTIONS

- What are three of your most concerning diagnostic measures and why?
- What is your strategy to address each one?

Business hygiene and insider risk

Business hygiene and insider risk have gained increasing importance over the past decade. We have seen the implementation of the U.S. Sentencing Commission's Federal Sentencing Guidelines for Organizations as well as the Sarbanes–Oxley Act and more aggressive corporate governance. There are a number of employable and measurable diagnostic indicators that may be combined to provide assurance that controls are effective or that red flags are present that warrant close scrutiny for corporate reputation (see Table 2.6). Simple examples include the absence of an embedded set of expectations (written policy) on business conduct and integrity overseen by clearly accountable managers, or differences in business unit treatment of misconduct. The criticality discussion above offers a particularly effective means of presenting and tracking internal criminal and business conduct trends. When used judiciously, the scorecard process is another effective means of tracking and illustrating how management addresses internal misconduct cases. The incident postmortems combined with other indices of inattention (background investigation results, information risk management, turnover statistics, etc.) all contribute to an assessment of a business unit's attention to an integrity-based work environment. Table 2.6 lists some common red flags for insider crime and internal misconduct and lists some corresponding diagnostic measures.

Table 2.6 Red Flags for Insider Crime and Internal Misconduct

Contributors to Insider Risk	Potential Diagnostic Measures
There are serious gaps in our safeguards. Anyone may be detected and exploited by empowered, trusted, and knowledgeable insiders.	• More aggressive audits on higher risk business processes • Security and internal audit address known vulnerabilities before the audit committee • Business units are measured for closing vulnerabilities and maintaining vigilance
Dependency on an incredibly complex, global technical environment The velocity of the business may mask control weaknesses.	• Performing routine risk analyses • Conformance with security policies • Measure employee security awareness • Increases in supervisory oversight lapses
There is evidence that the "honesty quotient" in the labor pool has declined.	• Results of thorough background reviews • Decreased candor in interviews
First line managers may not be aware or may not pay attention to the cues that indicate risky behavior and resulting exposure.	• Measured degree to which supervisors are attentive to cues that have been trained • Adequacy of planned risk management agenda is a part of performance review
Assignment of high-risk jobs to persons/ vendors of whom we know very little and the resultant failure to watch for "red flag" behavior.	• Results of background investigations • Adequacy of customized internal controls • Application of risk-based due diligence and contract provisions for vendors
Business units do not engage in sufficiently comprehensive risk analyses to proactively assure vulnerability awareness.	• More aggressive audits on higher risk business processes • Risk analysis part of business planning
Not enough done to share lessons learned among and across business units.	• Degree to which case studies shared in management training adequately frame real world deficiencies. • Proactive risk awareness programs
When concerns arise, escalation to management or control elements may not be timely.	• Culture rewards not shooting bearers of bad news and punishes cover-ups

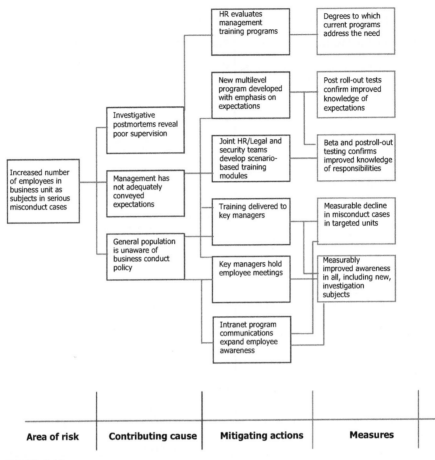

FIGURE 2.12

Measures mapping.

Measures mapping

Measures mapping is a visually interesting method of analyzing specific hazards or incidents to identify potential tactics. It is a modification of countermeasures mapping guidance utilized some years ago for licensees of the Nuclear Regulatory Commission. It takes the aggravating cause results of incident lessons-learned analyses as well as the high-level tasks identified to mitigate the risk and postulates corresponding measures or metrics for each countermeasure. This is a useful way to brief constituents on a proposed risk mitigation strategy and it enables status and cost updates in progress reporting. Figure 2.12 shows an example. Several other examples are included in Appendix 2.

Building a Model Appropriate to Your Needs

Introduction

In Chapter 1 we discussed how there is no singular model of "corporate security" and have also touched on many examples of a CSO's measurement and reporting objectives. Finding the model appropriate to your unique organizational culture, risk environment, and desires as a CSO or other security professional is your job. But this work also has a broader objective: to create a collaborative security community where professionals share ideas and support one another.

Does the business we are in make a difference?

Some people question whether the business we are in makes a difference. The answer is simple: absolutely. Whether you are in a regulated industry or one where security regulations are imposed, you have specific trends and events you should analyze and report to management. This includes risks to information security in health care, business continuity and reputation in financial services, physical security in energy or transportation, supply chain in food production, safety in transportation, and so forth. These risks are focal points for the security program in specific sectors but not to the exclusion of maintaining data on all applicable security elements. Consider the interdependencies among security programs we discussed in Chapter 1.

What are the most important data to the enterprise and its leaders?

Asking yourself about the most important data is an opportunity to identify the types of metrics the security organization needs to use in order to demonstrate value. The CFO should be consulted in determining an answer to this question. The CFO has established a presentation set that reflects key indicators unique to the corporation. Gain an understanding of how your metrics should be presented, to whom and on what frequency. Explore the sensitivity of the potential data, as that may color to whom it is distributed and how it is classified. This is especially true if shareholder confidence and reputational risk are in the equation. Other senior executives will be more interested in data and trends unique to their operations. The periodic exchange and analysis of data with governance team leaders is a particularly important and fruitful exercise. Internal audits routinely uncover vulnerabilities that contribute to risk that are also reflected in security incidents. This is especially true for data security, information protection, physical and logical access control, fraud risk, and business recovery planning. Legal counsel and human resources are routinely engaged (often with active investigative support from security) in a host of business conduct and employee relations issues. The opportunity to periodically stand back from this routine and examine incidents and trends typically offers insights to risk that would otherwise be lost. Risky management practices are identified, as is the need for policy reinforcement or creation. Collaborative relationships of vital importance to the security organization are built during these exercises.

TIPS FROM THE FIELD

Be extremely cautious about what information you exchange with whom and the accuracy of the data reported! When the security executive reports to senior management on cases, incidents, trends, and other sensitive matters, the data invariably illuminate deficiencies in one client department or another. Vultures will circle on a weakened colleague, the wrath of the CEO or other senior executive will rain down on a subordinate, all with the CSO's name attached to the consequences.

This is particularly true after a notable incident. Management wants and needs to know what happened and how it could have been prevented. Be straightforward with business partners who were involved that your findings and conclusions will be shared with top management. It goes without saying that the use of unverified or erroneous data that casts suspicion or a shadow on any business unit performance is a prescription for disaster.

THOUGHT QUESTION

- You have just sat down for your annual performance review discussion with the boss. He asks, "So, is the company more safe and secure this year than last as a direct result of your performance?" How would you answer him using some solid metrics as part of your story?

What are the most important data to the security executive?

What data are most important to the security executive depends on what is most important to your senior management and other stakeholders. It depends on what evaluative factors your supervisor will use to rate your performance. It depends on the kinds of measures or metrics that your company's shareholders and external pundits watch and utilize to judge the health and opportunity represented by your financial outlook. It depends on what you need to effectively measure the performance of your people and key vendors. It depends on what you need in your unique security environment to most effectively communicate, *influence*, and manage. Influence is often data dependent. Internally, the CSO's portfolio of services will determine the types of data needed for effective oversight and assessment of departmental and supervisory performance. Several metric categories appropriate to these services are discussed in the appendices.

If you have a good grounding in the business and have the right radar working, you likely know things about risk, the value equation, the competition, the business risk environment, and other potentially valued information that will not be available or obvious to other sources.

What should we measure?

The flip answer to the question "What should we measure?" is: Everything! However, remember Specific, Measurable, Attainable, Relevant, and Timely (SMART) metrics? We are not reporting on everything, but we need to stock the warehouse with the measures that support our programs. If resources (time, equipment, and dollars) are being allocated, management must assume we have measures to assess their performance. Following are some examples of a core set of measures.

Programs

In this context, "programs" refers to definable sets of planned activities for which performance expectations have been established. While they may be ongoing, like a background investigation program, they typically have a planned duration with key milestones and a conclusion where preestablished measures may be applied. Cycle times for the background process applied to each case or expectations of each investigator are examples. The cycle time is a financial expectation as well as an individual performance assessment in this example.

Change

A program structured to address a known risk must have a metric to guide planning, estimate the ROI, and permit assessment of progress toward the objective. Change measures provide the relationship of security programs to an improved state of risk management. An example would be:

The Facility A Security Department will reduce the incidence of (insert asset) thefts by 50% in the 4th quarter through a combination of increased employee awareness, more stringent access controls at all portals, improved CCTV coverage, and random searches of cleaning carts in the evening.

Public relations

Perceived excellence or soft spots are measurable with customer surveys, incident lessons-learned and case postmortems. Also, unsolicited feedback and managerial performance reviews reflecting on the performance of the security organization all serve to provide measured input.

People performance

The category of people performance is often missing in metrics discussions, although most employee performance programs involve numerical rating schemes. Performance assessment of security personnel, be they proprietary or contract, is perhaps the single most important element in the management of security resources.

Effective financial management

Effective financial management is a basic expectation of all managers. Cost management, including the ability to reduce cost while maintaining or increasing performance, demonstrates a favorable business connection particularly critical with service- or cost-centered functions.

THOUGHT QUESTIONS

- What security costs do you track now?
- Can you demonstrate that your initiatives have reduced the cost of security by reductions in risk rather than an outright reduction in security's budget?

Risk trends

Risk trends in business where the security organization has a stake in its mitigation or response will clearly involve measures of effectiveness or expectations by the affected business units. Annual loss expectancy may be an appropriate tool to estimate the cost of losses due to security incidents times the probability of the incident for the coming year, along with comparative results from prior years.

As noted in Chapter 2, the "hygiene" of the firm is a critical and often difficult measurement but the security organization (or the security committee) is in a unique position to identify and address emerging trends or potential inattention by line business managers. Examples are found in recruitment pools evidencing higher than normal derogatory background findings, increases in travel and entertainment expense fraud cases within specific business units, accident statistics, virus or technology abuse issues, or frequency of specific types of employee misconduct within employee groups or business units. Valuable red flags may be identified to alert specific individuals to risky trends that may be proactively addressed before they have more serious consequences. Examples might be increased workplace violence at specific facilities or times, frequent instances of inflated or false personal histories for employee candidates from a specific recruitment firm, or failures of business units to install software patches on a timely basis.

What happened?

After Action Reviews, or incident postmortems, often provide incredibly valuable measures of program and individual performance as well as revealing vulnerabilities in business process that may have gone unnoticed or unattended. Be honest in your assessment and engage all parties in the review. Doing so will ensure that mistakes are less likely to be repeated and also shows the commitment of the players to take the high ground for process improvement.

What are your objectives with these data?

In a 2006 SANS Institute paper titled "A Guide to Security," author Shirley Payne succinctly summarized the need for clear focus for the security executive interested in developing a security metrics program:

"Because developing and maintaining a security metrics program could take considerable effort and divert resources away from other security activities, it is critical that the goal(s) and objectives of the program be well defined and agreed upon up front. Although there is no hard and fast rule about this, a single goal that clearly states the end toward which all measurement and metrics gathering efforts should be directed is a good approach. A goal statement might be, for example:

Provide metrics that clearly and simply communicate how efficiently and effectively our company is balancing security risks and preventive measures, so that investments in our security program can be appropriately sized and targeted to meet our overall security objectives."[1]

What purpose will your work with measures and metrics serve? Metrics can be used to demonstrate one or more of the following:

- *Cost management*: For example, you should track a variety of cost elements for trends so that timely adjustments in expenses may be made, comparisons with peer operational costs may be drawn and the cost of various risk categories tracked to guide initiatives.
- *Risk management*: It is imperative that selected business risks be tracked to measure the effectiveness of safeguards and understand those risk dynamics that we know and those that are emerging. There are scores of potential risk management metrics. You have to select the few that are most meaningful to your organization.
- *ROI or value*: Where security's programs deliver reduced risk exposure and loss, they contribute to the bottom line. Where a business executive learns how to manage more effectively or with less risk, security's results are adding value for that manager and the organization. Where security enables the business to do something that the competition cannot, we are adding value. All of these benefits may be expressed in quantifiable terms.
- *Legal requirement*: Examples abound of metrics demonstrating conformance with a law, regulation, court order, or other legal purpose.

---

[1] "A Guide to Security Metrics," Shirley C. Payne, SANS Institute, June 2006, pg. 3–4, http://www.sans.org/reading-room/whitepapers/auditing/guide-security-metrics-55?show=guide-security-metrics-55&cat=auditing.

- *Policy requirement*: There are security policies. How well are they working? Where are the compliance issues and what are the consequences? Responses to these policies are measurable.
- *Life safety*: This involves huge mission issues with associated liability issues that security needs to monitor. Particular concerns are for incident response infrastructure, training and employee awareness, and relations with external first responders. Measures of effectiveness abound (see Appendix 1).
- *Internal influence*: Influence is one of the acknowledged measures of CSO effectiveness. Parts of Chapter 2 and multiple points of measure in Appendix 1 address this key concern.

Your security environment and corporate culture will significantly influence how you apply any of the potential measures. The wording is intended to give you ideas; you will need to modify the language to adapt to your objective. Some will require you to establish a baseline and then track positive or negative change. Others will simply report on a result you have selected to measure at some point. *Pick your few, not your many.*

Table 3.1 shows how a variety of measures may be categorized for results and tracked. Consider how these data might be translated into a positive story for your security organization. The selection of the business driver columns is yours and these are merely offered as examples that often are cited as relevant. You may want to limit these to one or two using an expanded right-hand column as space for elaboration and support for your selection.

Metrics can bite

Often, metrics can seem like a two-edged sword. Depending on the risk events you track, you need to recognize that these data are discoverable and will be the first documentation you are required to deliver if the company is sued for failing to protect in the face of known risk. Certain documents may be deemed attorney–client work papers. At a minimum, designated reports, trend analyses, and other metrics should be labeled for extremely limited distribution. Legal counsel should be consulted on the data that security will regularly track and should understand the beneficial risk management objectives of storing and analyzing the incident data.

Roles and responsibilities

Figure 3.1 displays the importance of roles and responsibilities for the security metrics program.

The pyramid in Figure 3.1[2] attempts to clearly show the critical importance of top-level support for the metrics program, as well as the importance of the role of the information system security officer in assuring accuracy of collected data.

---

[2]"IT Security Metrics Guidance, A Practical Approach to Measuring Information Security," Joan S. Hash, Tim Grance, National Institute of Standards and Technology.

Table 3.1 Categorized Measures Tracking

Security Measure or Metric	Business Drivers						
	Cost Management	Risk Management	ROI, Value	Legal Requirement	Policy Requirement	Life Safety	Internal Influence
Based on annual survey data, the quality of security's information results in actionable and measurable risk mitigation measures	•[a]	•	•				•
The number of life safety hazards proactively identified and successfully eliminated this year vs. past 3 years		•		•	•	•	•
Business processes with prior noted vulnerabilities or incident histories evidence measurable improvement after targeted security awareness programs		•					•
Minutes of critical system downtime this reporting period vs trend for past four quarters	•[a]	•	•				
Percentage of critical assets and functions for which the cost of compromise (loss, damage, disclosure, and disruption in access to) has been quantified	•	•	•		•		
Cycle times for four of five top priority security process improvements this year have been met or exceeded with reduced cost and increased customer satisfaction	•		•				•

[a]It is proposed that a risk potentially avoided translates to a cost containment result.

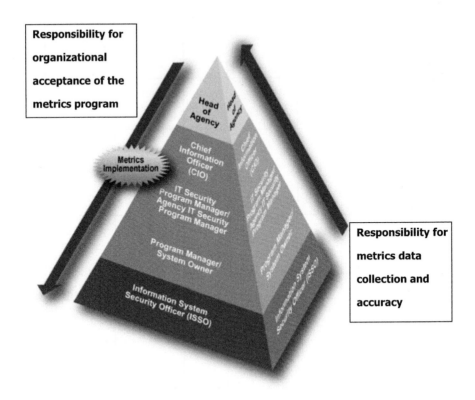

FIGURE 3.1

Responsibility for acceptance of a metrics program starts at the top.

Without the former, the ability to influence and effect change is doubtful. Without the latter, the credibility of the program and that of the security officer is irretrievably damaged. Those levels in between are accountable for taking those actions and the reporting routines required by the metrics.

It is unfortunately telling that the CSO is not portrayed in Figure 3.1. As noted earlier, those "other" security elements displayed in the figure play important roles in the protection of information assets and have accountability in service delivery to the chief information officer as well as reporting on metrics of impact to information risk management. In a revised view, the CSO at the bottom of this pyramid must engage and rely upon a similar upward chain of management, ultimately having secured the active support of the CEO.

How do I get the attention of different constituencies?

This discussion assumes the reader has effectively communicated with his or her internal customers (see Figure 3.2 for an example list of internal customers or

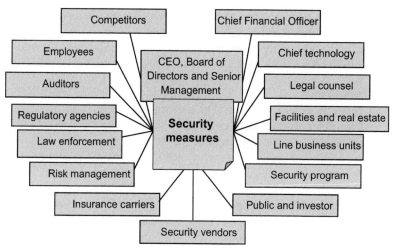

FIGURE 3.2

The many constituencies for security's measures and metrics.

constituencies) and they understand the suite of services offered by corporate security and have an understanding of at least the high level risks the security organization is addressing. If that is too great a stretch, then you likely have a bigger problem than trying to figure out a measures and metrics strategy!

Every internal client has something in the security space that keeps him or her awake at night. These are what we commonly refer to as "hooks"; that is to say, these are going to be of particular interest to the client and what we can use to get them to buy in or agree with the service(s) we are promoting. Hooks can be incidents that cause embarrassment, metrics that demonstrate the security measures they employ are working, or other indicators of positive or negative conditions. Timely and accurate reporting of security metrics, in a style and manner the client has specified, enables them to modify their business strategy to minimize the risk you are reporting. A spike in identity theft or a business outage in a certain region may require an aggressive customer outreach program, for example. Following are some potential hooks to consider as you query individual executives.

Reputational risk

Reputational risks can be franchise breakers and/or spell the end of an executive's career.[3] A cautionary tip at the right time will save the company in one way or another. Examples are the knowledgeable insider—the wrong guy in the right place; cyber crime, where customers are not safe doing business with your firm; the specter of

---

[3] The data you may be tracking may well be something that you want to share with a constituent as a clear warning sign in their road to fame and fortune. A cautionary tip at the right time will save the company in one way or another, and if that benefit changes behavior in someone who may not be paying attention, so be it.

regulatory sanctions owing to some noteworthy infraction; and a significant, or the protracted business interruption that causes the customer to go elsewhere. You know you have arrived at the point of reputational risk when you see the company's name on the upper right-hand corner of the *Wall Street Journal* and your share price plummeting.

Risky environment

Consider these potential scenarios: Your company is operating in places of high safety and corruption risk to your people and operations, or the external (or worse yet, the internal) infrastructure is unreliable, or the company relies on an aging suite of legacy hardware and applications, or you are hiring in a risky labor pool, or the company has outsourced critical business processes to firms that you know nothing about and there are no contractual obligations for secure operations. You might well find some executives who are counting the hours to the inevitable crisis. But you will find others that have not yet connected the dots to understand what awaits them. You can use a risky environment as a hook to draw them into the value of security metrics.

Do more with less

Where highly cost-effective business process performance is a core business driver, all service functions have to prove they are adding value. Be prepared to compare some measurable security component (like cost per square foot or cost per employee) with your competition, hopefully with favorable results. You may find that using proprietary vs contracted professional services for investigations or IT security services is more cost effective and all internal professional security services should be cost/performance evaluated annually against external vendors who maintain a level of responsiveness and quality comparable to corporate security.

Return on investment

ROI is about estimating cost of loss (of some valued element) vs cost of protection. The "easy" estimates are ones such as the intrusion or facility alarms that result in an interrupted break in or water incursion in a computer room. It is an interesting fact that many security executives do not know the real cost of protection because they do not track costs within client business units. How much time does that receptionist or LAN administrator spend on access control? The dilemma often presented to us by security professionals is how to measure value of a prevented incident where you have no firm evidence that an incident was really prevented. In the information security realm, firewall logs are intriguing resources, as are documented social engineering calls or forced entry incidents in electronic access control systems. How far would this event have gone and with what operational or financial impact if it continued? Depending on how management wants to structure ROI measures, the security executive needs to make sure they have the right types and reliability of data available. Cultivate a relationship with the CFO. They can often bring common sense to the exercise.

Corporate criminal liability

Look at the corporate meltdowns and falls from on high of the past few decades. You can definitely use examples of corporate criminal liability as a "hook," but work closely with general counsel if this is the hook you want to pursue to persuade management to invest in security. Use care and caution in the display of data that could be taken out of context. Develop a set of metrics collaboratively with the governance team, as this sharing will likely produce a more accurate picture of risk exposure.

The accountability model

Once a loss has occurred, some senior executives dispense with the risk event in short order and move to "Whose fault was this?" Proceed with caution here lest security becomes the company snitch, jeopardizing the trusting relationships you have formed with many client groups, especially the more risk-prone ones. That aside, risk reporting does rightfully involve a professional assessment of cause and effect. If there is a strong managerial accountability model at work, plan on addressing this question of blame and ensure that the targeted business executive(s) have taken reasonable steps to close the vulnerabilities that contributed to the security breach. You can then frame the postmortem in the most positive light.

How do we present the information to the target audience?

Earlier, we referred to the metrics display as a dashboard, like that found in an automobile. This is a good way to envision your customer/constituents' interests and view of the information you want to convey. Instead of temperature, oil pressure, and fuel level, you will select indicators meaningful to their operations. The key is focusing on a meaningful few rather than a dashboard akin to a complex instrument panel on an aircraft. For example:

- A graphical hook or two the customer wants to track on a consistent basis along with your analysis of the current state and what action security is taking to deal with apparent changes.
- A few of the more general metrics like cost of services or overall loss trends.
- Something based on a lesson learned here or elsewhere that the manager can take for the benefit of his or her operations. If the manager is someone who is a bit lax on testing their contingency plans, consider showing how a business unit recovered quickly owing to preparations and people knowing what to do because it was fresh. Postmortems on internal cases where the failure of internal controls are similar to vulnerabilities in this unit are sure to get the discussion going.

It is important that the presenter know their audience, be it one-on-one or before a group. It is wise to talk with someone who more routinely presents to your intended recipient and learn what has worked or failed for them in the past. Know the one or two takeaways you most want to get across and be prepared to be drilled on each one. If it is an update on certain metrics desired by a known constituency, be prepared to give your best interpretation of the data.

If you are presenting your annual budget proposal, use some selected metrics to demonstrate the need for new initiatives and a few to show the positive results from the past year. Financial support for a specific project requires a clear demonstration of the consequences of inaction and the cost benefits of support. Provide specific objectives that can be measured at established project milestones.

You will also need to carefully consider how you phrase your metrics. A cautionary example is presented at the beginning of Appendix 1. Briefly, you may desire to show a measured deficiency (e.g., percentage of servers in locations with uncontrolled physical access) or a positive (e.g., percentage of servers in locations with controlled physical access). Auditors and audit committees are going to be more interested in the former than the latter because of their concern for risk exposure. Many of the examples in Appendix 1 may be used in both ways depending on how you gather your data and focus on results.

Management of the data

This may all be well and good for the security organization with resources capable of gathering, collating, analyzing, and determining alternative ways to present focused data to a diverse array of customer needs. But what about the chief information security officer (CISO) who serves the IT organization exclusively and does not have access to physical security data? Or the security manager or director who currently owns physical security and investigations and is too busy to gather and collate data? Or the risk manager who somebody higher in management thinks has it all and does not need additional resources? These are the people who need to reach out and use all the tools at their disposal to get the job done.

THOUGHT QUESTIONS

- What data do you track that, in the wrong hands, could do damage to the company?
- Is it adequately protected?
- What additional protections should be employed?
- What security-related data routinely makes its way to the audit committee or other oversight group? If none, what risks are they missing that could come back to bite security?
- What should or could be done to ensure improved reporting at this level?

What tools are in the presentation toolkit?

In Chapter 1 of this book, we recommended that you find someone in your company who routinely works with the presentation of statistical information. You will likely find an experienced counselor in communications/marketing, finance, audit, or the IT department, all of whom typically work with graphical presentations. There are a variety of off-the-shelf tools available, but Microsoft Excel and PowerPoint will produce just about anything you might need. A great investment is to find a motivated administrative assistant or hourly employee who is trained in these products and can help you develop the presentation, and then spend some time with the counselor doing some hands-on work. Start slowly with those metrics that truly represent measures of demonstrated value—those that are truly SMART.

Interpreting the data

The process of interpretation likely begins with deciding what data you are going to gather and your objectives for its use. For example, understanding compliance with security policies is a key measure. But when you discover that something has happened in contravention of policy, you must ask, "Why was not it followed?" Your policy might require not less than an eight character log-in password mixing letters and numbers that is changed every 90 days. System administration reports may show significant noncompliance or invalid log-ins. Poor policy rollout, older workers, self-important "professionals," and those who have to remember multiple passwords may be the culprits, but you will have to dig to find the data. The stolen laptop problem discussed earlier had one fundamental cause in one location (doors propped open) and yet another (night cleaning crew and failure to properly store laptops after hours) in a different location. If you are tracking data to show change, such as desired reductions in specific incidents, you need to be able to establish a direct link to the "what" and "when" of step(s) taken in order to properly interpret the change.

We have alluded to the imperative of accuracy and understanding the real meaning of the data being presented. You bet metrics can bite! Jumping to conclusions, especially in an area like this, will destroy constituent confidence in security metrics. Do not gather the data if you do not intend to use it for a specific purpose, and *do not report it until you thoroughly understand what the data really means!* This is another important reason to conduct incident postmortems and employ lessons-learned analysis.

Organizing for success: engaging a security committee

It should be evident that security programs are *interdependent* and benefit from (if not rely on) strategic planning and program integration under single executive management. This fact argues in compelling ways for a full-service corporate security organization. If they are under separate organizational functions *and* there is no established means to share and analyze risk data, a consolidated view of security-related risk will be lost. The resulting picture of risk is likely very different than one that emerges from a single, coordinated source. This is too often a hard lesson learned from tragic or business-threatening circumstances.

If the consolidated model is not adopted, a security committee should be established and chartered by the CEO or chief operating officer (COO) and supported by corporate board of directors. Membership should include all senior executives engaged in managing the governance infrastructure and at least one senior executive from a business line. Where security programs are administered internally to a business unit[4] (fraud risk management and distributed information security functions are examples), they should be represented as well. If more broadly chartered, as with a governance committee, a security subcommittee should be established to more clearly gather and analyze risk exposure data unique to their functions. Typical membership of the security committee would include the CSO and senior management of corporate security, the CISO, the chief auditor, general counsel, the chief risk officer, compliance officer (where appropriate), HR employee relations, or a designee of HR engaged in business conduct matters. The business of the security committee should be to develop a set of results-oriented measures and related metrics that will:

- assist the board and senior management in understanding security-related risk and framing the parameters of risk tolerance;
- ensure that the dots are being effectively connected with regard to a reliable picture of risk exposure;
- enable follow-up recommendations and actions and track the results of risk mitigation activities; and
- provide a framework for assessing security's value as a core element of business strategy in an increasingly risky world.

What's next?

A brief exploration of the Internet will show that security metrics have evolved as almost the exclusive property of information security, yet we know that the territory of corporate security significantly transcends this limited area of enterprise risk management. This book is an initial step in responding to a wide range of security colleagues who indicated that a broader treatment of the subject was on their list of unmet needs. As a profession, we need to have a catalog of measures we can apply to our diverse programs to guide their development, delivery, and maximum value.

We want you to use this book as a starting point for ideas and notes on what works and what may not work in the development and application of measures and metrics in security. Ideally, this book will fall into the hands of nonsecurity professionals who have creativity, skills, and techniques transferable to our space and need. We also need to obtain feedback from business executives on what measures and metrics they need to see from their security managers. We hope it will be the success of our readers in better informing their management that will provide that feedback.

Do not be afraid to use this book as a workbook—test the ideas, concepts, and examples found in the chapters and appendices. Did they work? Why or why not? What were the results of success? How would you improve on them? What new examples have you found to work in specific areas of security operations? What

---

[4]As used throughout this book, a "business unit" is meant to encompass any subunit of a corporate or organizational structure such as a department or division, a separate company under a corporate umbrella, etc.

have you found that really grabs the attention of various constituents? The effort to improve security metrics and measures cannot stand on its own without the learning that comes from multiple business or public sector environments, all contributing to the diversity of risk environments, political challenges, and cultural or management styles. Together, we can create a model for corporate security organizations and leave a clear path for future generations to follow.

Appendix 1   Examples of Security-Related Measures and Metrics

The following tables are not intended to provide a comprehensive inventory of security-related measures and metrics. Rather, they are proposed as a prompt to stimulate thought, debate, and discussion appropriate to the unique organizational setting and purposes for which they will be utilized in your application. Many have been used in actual practice and have proven validity. You should not take them as is without truly making them relevant to your organization and what is important to your constituents. *These are starting points.*

The reader is encouraged to focus on developing a measures and metrics program that serves core business objectives, supports proactive risk management, and enables real assessment of the effectiveness and value of security programs and processes.

An important note: You will notice that some examples in the following tables are phrased in the negative to indicate a deficiency. For example: "vulnerabilities or control deficiencies identified in incident postmortems and reported to audit that remain unaddressed." Others clearly seek an affirmative response to indicate a positive state of affairs or accomplishments: "vulnerabilities or control deficiencies identified in incident postmortems and reported to audit that are positively resolved." Both are appropriate depending on the context of reporting and response sought and both impose a metric with different implications. In this example, the former is more informative than the latter, as it advises a potentially critical exposure.

The tables in each of the following sections are organized to enable the reader to assign each selected measure or metric to an associated business driver in the following sample fashion. Each of the following measures, indicators or metrics will have some relationship to one or more of the elements found in the seven columns at the right. This connection is valuable in aligning the measure and its associated security program element with an accepted business principle, legal requirement or program benefit. Ideally, we may collectively edit and add to this list thereby building a more diverse and dynamic metrics data base. Some duplication may occur due to similarity of objective.

Example

Security Measure or Metric	Business Drivers						
	Cost Management	Risk Management	ROI, Value	Legal Requirement	Policy Requirement	Life Safety	Internal Influence
No. nuisance alarms from corporate facilities monitored by corporate security	X	X				X	
Security cost as a percentage of total company revenue	X		X				
No. safety hazards proactively identified and eliminated annually		X		X	X	X	
Percentage of critical information assets or functions residing on systems that are currently in compliance with approved system architecture		X			X		X
No. failed or ineffectual business unit responses to issues identified by security as control weaknesses that result from fraud prevention analysis, investigations, or other feedback		X					X

It is hoped that the results of this approach will assist the chief security officer in focusing on the selection of specific measures or metrics that best serve the demonstration of business responsiveness and perceived value.

Key Performance and Risk Indicators	Cost Management	Risk Management	ROI, Value	Legal Requirement	Policy Requirement	Life Safety	Internal Influence
Annual percentage of interrupted business processes that were satisfactorily restored within targeted timelines							
Incident [type] cost as a percent of (a) revenue, (b) occupancy, or (c) cost of operation							
Percentage of risk assessment recommendations accepted and implemented year by year							
Percentage of vulnerability assessment findings that have not been cleared since last reporting period by potential consequence of findings							
Percent of vulnerability findings for which root cause analysis and testing have confirmed successful risk mitigation							
Percent of vulnerability findings for which methods of exploitation were generally known within the resident workforce							
Percent of critical business process with current risk assessments							
Percent of critical business process with current risk assessments where all approved remedial actions have been completed							
Rate of change for frequency and severity of security infractions, accidents, crime, or other *preventable* risk events							
Internal misconduct and security policy violations per X no. employees							

Continued

Key Performance and Risk Indicators	Cost Management	Risk Management	ROI, Value	Legal Requirement	Policy Requirement	Life Safety	Internal Influence
Percent on-time delivery of annual plan objectives							
Percent of test subjects who after 12 months of service retain principal elements of security responsibilities delivered in security orientations							
Percent of regulatory requirements that are deemed in compliance (noncompliance) by the governing body							
Percent conformance of budgeted activities to annual plan							
WPV incidents per X no. employees at various locations and types of business operations							
Trend for penetrations of networks by hackers or criminals							
Percentage of information security program elements for which approved policies and controls are operational							
Percent of employee hotline calls for fraud or policy violations vs peer sector average							
Percentage of incidents that result in damage, compromise, or loss beyond established thresholds							
Percentage of incidents of internal misconduct resulting in termination and/or referral for restitution and/or prosecution							
Percentage of incidents that exploited known vulnerabilities with known solutions							

Percentage clearance of notable, unresolved security-related audit findings reported to the Audit Committee or regulatory body				
Quarterly/Annual year by year management of budget to plan on an acceptability scale of 1–5				
Quarterly/Annual year by year contract guard force performance on an acceptability scale of 1–5				
Overall incident response quarterly/annual year by year on an acceptability scale of 1–5				
Customer service measured Quarterly/Annual year by year on an acceptability scale of 1–5				
Security technology management operations measured Quarterly/Annual year by year on an acceptability scale of 1–5				
Investigation outcomes measured Quarterly/ Annual year by year on an acceptability scale of 1–5				
No. common security defects found in each reporting period across multiple locations and/ or business processes				
Severity of security defects uncovered by proactive investigation, audit, or after-action analysis				
Percent of security policies that are accepted and endorsed by senior management				
Key risk indicators found in business units based on security inspections				
Six Sigma—Failure modes and effects analysis in four potentially consequential types of security incidents				

Continued

—cont'd

Key Performance and Risk Indicators	Cost Management	Risk Management	ROI, Value	Legal Requirement	Policy Requirement	Life Safety	Internal Influence
Characteristics of product thefts by period of time							
Response time to customer-determined resolution of issues reported to confidential line							
Percentage of confidential line calls founded/unfounded with allegations of terminable misconduct							
Percentage positive supervisory evaluation and substantive acceptance of incident/investigation report on first draft							
Hours to close investigation vs comparative complexity and plan threshold for type							
Comparative results of closed investigations by investigator							
Assessment of physical access control based upon challenge response							
Tested effectiveness of business unit personnel in implementing security procedures							
Percentage tested readiness of contingency or disaster recovery plans							
Effective planning, deployment, and testing of security technology affirms high probability of detection and reduced response times							
Depth of planning and quality of response affirmed in minimal disruption and fast recovery from incidents							
Measurably effective security countermeasures support regulatory compliance and defense against litigation							
Postincident measurement of customer confidence in security controls							

Percentage change in frequency and/or severity of security infractions, accidents, crime, or other *preventable* risk events				
Percentage change in derogatory BI rates in specific hiring populations				
Percentage change in security process cycle times such as software patching				
Percentage change in distribution of sensitive business assets to known higher risk locations				
Percentage change in engagement of essential internal relationships in matters of security interest				
Percentage change in imposed budget reductions made without consideration of increased risk				
Comparative trends of derogatory background findings in selected categories of persons with access				
Impact of increased unemployment on BI findings				
Assessment of management concern regarding adverse findings of offshore due diligence				
Impact of security awareness programs on top 50 business units owning A-1 critical processes				
Status of security business plans within selected operational centers				
Percentage compliance with contractual security requirements for five key supply chain partners				
Assessment of impact of increased deployment of security technology vs security manpower				

Continued

Key Performance and Risk Indicators	Cost Management	Risk Management	ROI, Value	Legal Requirement	Policy Requirement	Life Safety	Internal Influence
Guard tour performance for top 100 most critical tour points							
Postawareness program percentage increase in knowledge of security policy							
Percentage change in travel itinerary or adopted safeguards after risk briefings							
Percentage of facilities capable of isolation and secure operations post-biohazard incident							
Percentage effectiveness of mail security operations based on bypass testing							
No. employee days lost to health and safety issues and/or violations							
Percentage of designated first responders trained and qualified in required response procedures							
Increases or decreases in average time to re-move logical and physical access credentials							
Year by year trend in internal misconduct per 1000 (100?) trusted insiders							
Percentage of security incidents for which root cause analysis was conducted by severity category							
Percentage of security incidents by severity category whose root cause was attributable to failure of a physical security control							
Percentage of security incidents by severity category whose root cause was attributable to failure of a personnel security control							
Percentage of security incidents by severity category whose root cause was attributable to failure of an IT security control							

Percentage of security incidents by severity category whose root cause was attributable to failure of an operational security control					
Security incidents per 1000 persons in the service population by location					
Percentage of security incidents by severity category whose root cause was attributable to failure of a combination of security controls					
No. security defects identified by period by proactive risk assessment and eliminated as confirmed by test					
No. security defects identified by, period by proactive risk assessment that failed to be eliminated within the specified period by severity of potential consequences					
Percentage of security incidents for which a response time goal was specified that (a) met or exceeded the goal or (b) failed to meet the goal					
Ratio (or Percentage) of cost of loss to cost of protection					
Percentage of security incidents for which a response time goal was specified that failed to meet the goal					
No. employees at risk as a percentage of total employee population assigned to site					
Total physical security expense as a percentage of (a) property value or (b) occupancy cost					
Regulatory Compliance					
Pass/fail rate from government-conducted security inspections (keyed to program life cycle)					
Rates of compliance or noncompliance for sites where policies have been communicated and enforced					

Continued

Key Performance and Risk Indicators	Cost Management	Risk Management	ROI, Value	Legal Requirement	Policy Requirement	Life Safety	Internal Influence
Regulatory Compliance							
Percent reduction in business impact assigned to approved alternatives for mandated security measures							
Reduction in insurance cost attributable to carrier acceptance of safeguard effectiveness							
Response time to special access area alarms in excess of mandated threshold							
Potential for fine/sanction eliminated by proactive risk assessment or inspection							
Percent of personnel submitted for clearance found to have material derogatory backgrounds							
Percent of programs with tested conformance of safeguards and internal controls							
No. reportable security defects found in outsourced suppliers per audit or inspection							
Percentage of compromise incidents where compromise is ruled out vs in							
Percentage of control deficiencies identified as a percent of total controls in the safeguard process							
Percentage of control deficiencies reported to owner and confirmed as resolved by test							
Elimination of sanctionable penalties associated with frequency and severity of compliance deviations							
Percent change in background derogatory rates for persons with access/by program							
No. unauthorized persons found in controlled space per period							

Cost of resolution of data spills by business unit per period				
Security cost as a percent of total program revenue				
Relationship of entities inspected and security defects found				
No. of unaccounted laptops with encryption disabled				
No. of defective or unsecure physical access controls found by tours per 24h period				
No. of false or nuisance alarms per protected area per 24h period				
Percentage (or No. hours per period) of false/nuisance alarms requiring a posted security officer until cause is resolved				
Average time to clear identified control deficiencies				
No. of information protection violations per 100 employees				
No. of incidents past month/quarter having a low, moderate, or severe impact on business unit operations or profitability				
Percentage of founded cases closed by re-covery, sanction, or predefined measure of successful outcome				
No. reported violations of policies related to conduct or security of [Co.] assets				
Percentage of total incidents with quantifiable losses per quarter				
Percentage security controls assessed this quarter determined to be compliant				
Percentage of investigated crimes cleared by arrest, sanction, or recovery				

Continued

Key Performance and Risk Indicators	Cost Management	Risk Management	ROI, Value	Legal Requirement	Policy Requirement	Life Safety	Internal Influence
Regulatory Compliance							
Percentage Security Plan objectives on performance target, cost, and schedule							
Fines from self-reported and regulator-initiated security defects							
Mean time to mitigate critical vulnerabilities [as confirmed by test]							
Crimes against people and property/threat reports from IAITF, an international risk association							
Award fees achieved compared to total fee potential							
Notices of corrective actions required by regulators as a percentage of no. inspections for the period							
Percent conformance with following elements of compliance management							
A qualified, accountable party to oversee the compliance program							
Periodic risk assessment process aligned with regulatory focus							
Process for confidential reporting of noncompliance							
Verifiable reporting upward and externally as required							
Communication of program to engage and empower employees							
Metrics to demonstrate degrees of compliance							
Measurable risk mitigation plans funded and active							

Measures of Customer Satisfaction with Security				
Demonstrated willingness to open doors to independent review of controls				
Customer satisfaction survey indicates work with corporate security was successful				
Support for security programs and initiatives is demonstrated in survey results				
Indicators of business understanding of security:				
Percentage of proposed security policies signed off, endorsed, and advocated by senior management				
Percentage of total security breaches involving senior managers				
Percentage of security initiatives incorporated in business plans at security's initiative				
Percent of individuals assigned within restricted or limited access areas who demonstrate adequate levels of security policy awareness and individual responsibility				
Instances (No.) where the business champions security (correspondence, comments, etc.)				
Percentage of candidates not hired due to BI findings				
Percentage of third-party relationships avoided or terminated because of due diligence review				
Managers are encouraged to seek out vulnerabilities in business process				
Managers are well informed on control deficiencies or cues to risky behavior				

Continued

Key Performance and Risk Indicators	Cost Management	Risk Management	ROI, Value	Legal Requirement	Policy Requirement	Life Safety	Internal Influence
Measures of Customer Satisfaction with Security							
Percentage adherence to physical security controls (visible credentials, locked doors, etc.)							
Key indicators of security's understanding of the business:							
Percentage attendance by the business at the selected security training programs							
No. meetings and frequency with key stakeholders, partners, or customers							
No. high risk processes "walked through" for proactive risk identification							
No. planning meetings about the business and its future (3–5 year, etc.)							
No. engagements in key product launches, processes, relationships							
Indicators of business unit willingness/ reluctance to escalate concerns on integrity or misconduct issues							
Percent of business units that independently test their security controls and report results							
Acceptance of security is high/low and accountability for security is excellent/minimal							
Willingness to involve and cooperate with corporate security in matters affecting the company							
Compliance with security policy (protection of proprietary information, access control, etc.).							
The percentage of applications/platforms without adequate identification, authentication, authorization, confidentiality, data integrity, nonrepudiation, and administration							

The deployment of software or systems without being vetted for adequate security features or safeguards					
No. requests for security team's services—extent of consulting					
Percentage of indicators from incident postmortems demonstrating business sharing of security responsibility					
Percentage of visible signs of credentials being worn or not worn, documents being appropriately labeled or not labeled, etc.					
Indicators of failure to address repeated security violations by type					
No. instances where management made changes to processes, products, or relationships where there was a security risk impact without security consultation					
Hiring of personnel after receipt of derogatory background information from security					
Engagement of outside business relationship after receipt of derogatory information from security					
No. SEC, regulatory, or other investigative inquiries relating to matters within the purview of corporate security's mission					
Adverse publicity within the purview of corporate security's charter					
The existence of demonstrated business unit loss history with no corresponding attentive response					
Percentage acceptance or failure to accept recommendations of the security organization					

Continued

Key Performance and Risk Indicators	Cost Management	Risk Management	ROI, Value	Legal Requirement	Policy Requirement	Life Safety	Internal Influence
Measures of Customer Satisfaction with Security							
Percentage of incident postmortems resulting in known and unaddressed vulnerabilities and risks							
Percentage of incident postmortems resulting in previously unknown vulnerabilities and risks							
Presence of exploitable vulnerabilities to [designate] critical business process							
Outsourced business processes with sensitive information or other valuable assets where no risk due diligence was performed							
Due diligence for integrity or other reputational risk issues are performed							
Percentage of backgrounds of personnel in [designate] sensitive positions are completed with all outstanding issues satisfactorily adjudicated							
Percentage of all personnel with known derogatory background retained after no-hire recommendation from security							
Internal investigations indicate management practices to punish or discount messengers of bad news							
Incident and Administrative Cost Data							
Reduction in case cost by type per period							
Security cost contribution to overhead rate							
Value of customer losses to security events							
Cost (or Percentage) of security staff time directed to security vs nonsecurity activities							
Hours of security personnel directly assignable to security incident management as a percentage of total hours available							

Cost of definable in-sourced vs outsourced security activity to documented standard						
Cost per day of time by employees to selected security processes by distributed sampling						
Cost of investigations per business unit as a percentage of their annual revenue (or cost)						
Security cost as a percent of total program revenue						
Total physical security expense as a percentage of (a) property value or (b) occupancy cost						
Employee (served population) headcount per security (or protective operations) employee						
Security cost per square foot of space under protection (or cost per square foot of assets monitored)						
Percent conformance of budgeted activities to annual plan						
Increase/decrease in percentage of total incidents with quantifiable losses per quarter						
Recovery time converted into $ saved or lost $/min						
Cost of protection as a percentage of maximum foreseeable loss (enterprise, revenue-center or site-specific)						
Key Financial Performance Measures						
Reduced security cost to revenue-generating programs						
Annual cost of loss to various categories of incidents compared to annual cost of protection measures						

Continued

Key Performance and Risk Indicators	Cost Management	Risk Management	ROI, Value	Legal Requirement	Policy Requirement	Life Safety	Internal Influence
Key Financial Performance Measures							
Fraud claims per X no. transactions							
Cost of investigation vs value of loss							
Increase/decrease in security cost per site per annum							
Cost of BI as a percentage of total on-boarding (staffing) process							
Security cost associated with providing access to trusted systems/applications by third parties							
Cost of investigations less recoveries as a percentage of total losses							
Cost of business continuity operations compared to cost of downtime to business interruption							
Benchmarked cost data for similar/equivalent peer group operations							
Cost of recovery vs planned threshold of loss							
Cost of resolution of data spills by business unit per period							
Cost of investigation and replacement of employee terminated for security-related cause							
Cost benefit of quantifiable security programs							
Reduced insurance cost assignable to affirmed safeguard effectiveness							
Reduction in insurance cost attributable to carrier acceptance of safeguard effectiveness							
Value for fine/sanction eliminated by proactive risk assessment or inspection							

Security-related award fees achieved compared to total fee potential			
Value of security program contribution to contracts won			
Reduction of quantifiable losses attributable to cost-responsive safeguards			
Rate of change for frequency and severity of security infractions, accidents, crime, or other preventable risk events			
Elimination of quantifiable costs associated with required security controls			
Value of savings attributable to reduction in labor intensive security controls via technology application			
Cost avoidance attributable to elimination of exploitable vulnerabilities			
Savings attributable to reduced cycle times that eliminate business process delay			
Demonstrated impact on insurance rates based upon measurable security program effectiveness			
Value of time recovered by elimination of a required security process or reduced cycle time			
Critical process recovery time converted to $ saved or $/min			
Ratio of business continuity operations cost to cost of downtime to business interruption			
Reduced security cost to revenue-generating programs			
Vulnerabilities identified and mitigated (quantifiable costs avoided) via proactive risk assessment and previously unidentified risks mitigated via incident postmortems			

Continued

—cont'd

Key Performance and Risk Indicators	Cost Management	Risk Management	ROI, Value	Legal Requirement	Policy Requirement	Life Safety	Internal Influence
Key Financial Performance Measures							
Reduction of quantifiable losses attributable to cost-responsive safeguards							
Elimination of quantifiable costs associated with required security controls							
Reduction in labor intensive security controls via technology application							
No. security violations involving cleared employees per violation opportunities (in place)							
Reduction of cost associated with supply chain logistics							
Security program contribution to contracts won							
Defect rates of key protection processes							
Reduced cycle times that eliminate business process delay							
Quantifiable impact of exploitable and unaddressed vulnerabilities							
Award fees for safeguard program goal achievement							
Reduced insurance cost assignable to affirmed safeguard effectiveness							
Reduced risk attributable to timeliness of response on-site vs off-site resources							
Cost of protection as a percentage of maximum foreseeable loss							
Reduced time to critical full business process recovery							
Proactive elimination of security, safety, and business continuity hazards							
Claims against organization (or security vendors) for inadequate or negligent security							

Recovery time converted into $ saved or lost $/min				
Cost of proprietary security service vs contracted equivalent				
Cost of case by (type, location, investigator, etc.)				
Increased/decreased cost of insurance premiums resulting from assessment of safeguards effectiveness or loss event(s)				
Cost of investigations less recoveries as a percentage of total losses				
Benchmarked cost data for similar/equivalent peer group operations				
Total cost of loss (less recovery)				
Lost income loss				
Cost of temporary substitution and/or replacement				
Offset from insurance claim				
Demonstrated impact on insurance rates based upon measurable security program effectiveness				
Write-off loss				
Cost of critical business process downtime				
Cost of backup spares or facilities, redundant capabilities, and relocation costs				
Employee (served population) headcount per protective operations employee				
Cost of business continuity operations compared to cost of downtime to business interruption				

Continued

Key Performance and Risk Indicators	Cost Management	Risk Management	ROI, Value	Legal Requirement	Policy Requirement	Life Safety	Internal Influence
Key Financial Performance Measures							
Annual cost of loss to various categories of incidents compared to annual cost of protection measures							
Cost of recovery vs planned threshold of loss							
Exposure vs actual loss							
Incident cost—external—fraud							
Incident cost—external—criminal							
Incident cost—internal—criminal							
Incident cost—internal—business conduct							
Incident cost—internal—accidents resulting in claims							
Incident cost—internal—computer, technology abuse, info security violations							
Incident cost—internal—inventory shrinkage							
Local police crime statistics for each property							
Uniform crime reports for corporate locations							
Data from internally generated crime risk analyses							
Prosecution referrals (no. by year, success rates, type, other)							
Employee discipline—(by time period, by business unit, by type)							
CapRisk data for individual addresses							
Complaint trends from employees and others on-site							
Industry data on security-related trends							
Accidents attributable to employee action vs not attributable							

Metric						
Accident per mile compared to peers						
Fraud claims per X no. transactions						
Reported crimes per square foot of operational space (leased vs owned)						
Penetration delay time (container, facility construction, etc.)						
Security Awareness						
Employee or target population security awareness increases based on information communicated						
Business processes with prior noted vulnerabilities or incident histories evidence measurable improvement after targeted security awareness programs						
No. business unit security education and awareness briefings or postinspection assists conducted						
Percentage of tested population having accurate knowledge and awareness of accountable security procedures						
Percentage of person trips with risk assessments for travel to high risk locations						
Percentage of exercises and drills indicate appropriate levels of knowledge and awareness						
Audit Implications						
Significant/notable audit findings within client business processes with security-related implications						
Resolved/cleared per business unit						
Unresolved/uncleared per business unit						
Significant/notable audit findings within the corporate security program(s)						

Continued

Key Performance and Risk Indicators	Cost Management	Risk Management	ROI, Value	Legal Requirement	Policy Requirement	Life Safety	Internal Influence
Audit Implications							
Resolved/cleared per business unit							
Unresolved/uncleared per business unit							
Unresolved or unaddressed security-related audit findings reported to the Audit Committee							
Vulnerabilities or control deficiencies identified in incident postmortems and reported to audit that have been resolved							
Vulnerabilities or control deficiencies identified in incident postmortems and reported to audit that remain unaddressed							
Severity of security defects uncovered by proactive investigation, audit, or after-action analysis							
Percentage of required internal and external information security (other security program) audits completed and reviewed by the Board							
Percentage of key external requirements for which the organization has been deemed by objective audit or other means to be in compliance							
Percentage of identified risks that have a defined risk mitigation plan against which status is reported in accordance with policy							
Percent of security policies that are accepted and endorsed by senior management							
Background Investigations							
No. personnel not processed through a background check prior to hire							
No. derogatory backgrounds in specific employment pools, over time							

No. personnel retained with (cautionary) BIs					
No. personnel retained with (terminable) BIs					
Case completion and cycle time rates for background case analysts					
BI cost per case (by location, business unit, recruitment pool, employee category, etc.)					
Percent of posthire terminations for cause having no BI or hire in spite of adverse background recommendations					
BI adjudication results and days to close					
Percentage of candidate-executed personal history statements found to contain material discrepancies per reporting period and by recruitment pool					
Case ageing rates for HR staffing teams					
Percentage of BIs completed within targeted timeline					
Post-internal vetting and submittal time to complete government agency BI process					
Percentage of persons hired with adverse suit-ability findings					
Trends for increased rates of derogatory background information in specific hiring populations					
Percentage of employee applicants rejected for hire where access to [Co.] sensitive, restricted, or confidential information may be granted					
No. vendor due diligence examinations with relationships confirmed, modified, or avoided					
Percentage drug test pass/fail rates by business unit and location					

Continued

Key Performance and Risk Indicators	Cost Management	Risk Management	ROI, Value	Legal Requirement	Policy Requirement	Life Safety	Internal Influence
Background Investigations							
Prehire workplace mandated drug testing:							
No. tested with test trends:							
Percentage of test-negative/test-positive							
Test-positives dismissed immediately							
Test-positives referred for counseling and treatment							
Test-positives reassigned to other duties							
Test-positives placed on probation or suspension							
Third-Party Due Diligence Examination							
No. relationships established without a due diligence investigation							
Percent of third-party relationships wherein the contract docs incorporate measurable security requirements, policies, and procedures appropriate to the level of risk exposure of the relationship							
Derogatory findings from postcontract award examination							
Affirmed/supported from postcontract award examination							
Case completion rates for due diligence investigators							
No. relationships by finding:							
Affirmed/supported							
Avoided							
Substantive modification to mitigate identified risk							
Terminated							

Examination results by:				
Type of risk identified				
Location–country, state, county, city, etc.				
Type of vendor service				
Size of business				
Contract value				
Vendor name				
Companies with similar ownership				
Business unit owing the relationship				
Business Conduct and Reputational Risk				
Rates of internal crime or misconduct per 1000 employees				
No. terminations for cause as a percent of employee population				
No. employees involved as subjects of investigations as a percentage of the total employee population				
No. internal investigation subjects who indicate a lack of knowledge of the policy they are accused of violating				
No. security incidents caused by now-terminated employees/vendors				
No. security incidents attributable to employees where HR has not informed security				
No. hostile workplace incidents within specific organizational units				
No. technology abuse incidents (banned internet site access, information security violations, time abuse, etc.) within specific organizational units				

Continued

Key Performance and Risk Indicators	Cost Management	Risk Management	ROI, Value	Legal Requirement	Policy Requirement	Life Safety	Internal Influence
Business Conduct and Reputational Risk							
No. HR/employee relations referrals with later WPV or threats of violence (if available from HR)							
No. founded and unfounded calls to the (sentencing guidelines or Sarbanes) confidential line							
No. failed or ineffectual business unit responses to issues identified as control weaknesses that result from fraud prevention analysis, investigations, or other							
Reliance on complex technical environment with significant uptime reliability							
Business operations in higher risk areas (locally, offshore)							
Presence of critical business process							
Known local risks (bribery, extortion, trade secrets, etc.)							
Company risk and criticality ranked business process							
Process for incident postmortems to record learning and eliminate risks							
No. findings brought to security by managers encouraged to seek out vulnerabilities in business process							
Managers are well informed on control deficiencies or cues to risky behavior							
Presence of exploitable vulnerabilities to [designate] critical business process							
Outsourced business processes with sensitive information or other valuable assets outside of company control							

Due diligence for integrity or other reputational risk issues are performed				
Backgrounds of personnel in [designate] sensitive positions are completed				
Percent of personnel with known derogatory background issues that are hired				
Tendency to shoot messengers of bad news				
Business unit reluctance to escalate concerns on integrity or misconduct issues				
No means for confidential reporting of wrongdoing or other issues				
Criminal Incidents and Investigations				
Cost of investigations per capita				
Investigative case aging				
Cost of investigations per business unit as a percentage of their revenue (or cost)				
Investigations per investigator				
Case closures with results per investigator				
Recoveries per investigator				
Postcase feedback from business unit clients (include per lead investigator)				
Statistical increases in internal and external investigative matters overall				
Statistical increases in internal and external investigative matters per organizational unit				
Investigative Priority:				
Value of loss				
Impact on business operations				
Impact on reputation				

Continued

Key Performance and Risk Indicators	Cost Management	Risk Management	ROI, Value	Legal Requirement	Policy Requirement	Life Safety	Internal Influence
Criminal Incidents and Investigations							
Timeliness of reporting the incident							
Likelihood of solving the case (solvability factors)							
Likelihood of asset recovery							
Case complexity/simplicity							
Organizational politics							
Likelihood of restitution							
Cost of investigation vs value of loss							
Management appetite for referral to prosecution							
Percentage of cases taken to successful prosecution							
Percentage of cases handled in-house vs outsource							
Percentage of case closures with measurably beneficial results for each party							
Quality of investigative postmortems for identification of causal factors that lead to closure of vulnerability/measurable reduction of risk exposure							
The percentage of suspicious transactions that have high probability factors for money laundering							
Security Operations, Physical Security, and Premises Protection							
Square feet space of business operations in countries or locations outside security resources or oversight							

Frequency of travel to, or permanent location of work in, high risk foreign locations			
No. nuisance alarms reported from executive residences dependent upon the time to police response			
Measured rates of alarm system effectiveness			
No. nuisance alarms from corporate facilities monitored by security			
Uptime reliability of critical alarm system components			
Frequency of system component maintenance with associated failure rates			
Mean time between failures			
Mean time to repair			
Vendor-specific failure rates			
Vendor-specific response time to repair or replacement			
Deployment of diverse and redundant protective elements where notably critical or targeted assets are the object of protection			
Safeguards (2 person rules, etc.) for critical protective system activation			
Access Control Administration			
Percentage of found contraband from random bag searches			
Security of badge credential blanks			
Percentage trained receptionist/gatekeepers in higher risk areas			
Percentage successful unchallenged/uncontrolled access to higher risk spaces			

Continued

—cont'd

Key Performance and Risk Indicators	Cost Management	Risk Management	ROI, Value	Legal Requirement	Policy Requirement	Life Safety	Internal Influence
Access Control Administration							
Percentage of HR who inform of termination timeliness							
Percentage of tests of mail screening procedures deemed meeting detection standard							
Percentage of unauthorized access attempts by risk-ranked portal							
Secure Areas (Specifically designated spaces assigned for most sensitive operations and provided with above norm physical and operational safeguards):							
No. successful intrusions or losses to outsider adversaries							
No. successful intrusions or losses to insider adversaries							
No. successful compromises of closely held security measures by insiders							
Penetration delay time for access to targeted assets in unattended secure areas							
Penetration delay time for access to targeted assets in attended secure areas							
Mean time to respond to intrusion in unattended secure area							
Cost per square foot for closely controlled secure vs normal business spaces							
Protective Security Operations							
Hours of preassignment training							
Hours of postassignment training							

No. security vulnerabilities identified and reported by proactive patrol or other operational procedures			
Overtime rates by location, shift, individual, business unit			
Overtime charged or attributable to security incidents by type or location			
Life Safety			
No. safety-related incidents annually over time			
No. claims for injury by employees, visitors, others			
No. hazards proactively identified and eliminated per reporting period			
No. false fire alarms resulting in business interruption/evacuation			
Security systems—false alarm rates (by premises or other criterion)			
Local fines paid for false alarms directed to local police departments			
Floor wardens per employee by location			
Drill frequency compared to best practice standard by type			
WPV (by type, location, perpetrator, victim			
Response time			
By internal first responders to criminal/other incident call for service			
Response time goal by location or type			
By qualified emergency medical technicians			

Continued

Key Performance and Risk Indicators	Cost Management	Risk Management	ROI, Value	Legal Requirement	Policy Requirement	Life Safety	Internal Influence
Life Safety							
Defibrillators have been deployed in key locations and individuals trained							
By external as compared to internal qualified first responders by location and time							
Vehicle-related risks							
Vandalism/theft from vehicle							
Suspicious vehicle							
Unauthorized parking—visitor or employee							
Stolen vehicle from company property							
Bioterrorism							
Plans in place to address biohazards							
Percent of facilities surveyed for risk exposure							
Percent of facilities capable of isolation and secure operations							
Percent of facilities with prepositioned response resources							
Percent of internal first responders trained in biohazard detection and response							
Ability to identify all personnel in facility at time of suspected exposure							
Demonstrated effectiveness of mail screening safeguards							
Availability of trained and properly equipped public first responders							
Time for trained first responders to respond to potential hazard							

Percent of test objects correctly identified				
Demonstrated ability of local resources to positively identify suspected substance within a planned timeline				
Unified incident command protocols and facilities in place and tested				
Executive Protection				
Increases/decreases in travel of (high profile) employees to high risk locations				
Increases/decreases in security-related events at high risk locations				
Percentage of briefed executives accepting tailored protection [at home] [in travel]				
Internal Revenue Service (IRS) required fees for protective services delivered to employees				
Historical trends in travel risk briefings				
Increases/decreases in engagement of protective services for traveling executives				
The extent to which security is engaged in the planning and delivery of public or semipublic events involving high profile executives				
Increases/decreases in no. requests for security presence at selected executive events				
Key executive protection/crisis management plans in place and exercised involving essential personnel				
Percentage of trips canceled or significantly adjusted based on a recommendation from the EP team (risk avoidance)				
Percentage of executive protection (EP) supported trips that occur without a significant issue (risk avoidance)				

Continued

Key Performance and Risk Indicators	Cost Management	Risk Management	ROI, Value	Legal Requirement	Policy Requirement	Life Safety	Internal Influence
Executive Protection							
Percentage of trips where the EP team had to intercede on behalf of the traveling executive (direct ROI)							
Percentage of trips where the EP team is not initially engaged but is activated midtrip based on a specific event (costs could have been reduced if EP was engaged at outset)							
Percentage of trips where the EP team is consulted and provides risk mitigation advise, but does not deploy operationally (value added at a low cost)							
Workplace Violence							
WPV policy, response plans and interdepartmental team(s) are in place							
WPV incidents per 1000 employees							
WPV incidents per 1000 employees compared to peer group							
No. incidents satisfactorily concluded/resolved							
No. employees with domestic restraining orders							
No. HR cases involving allegations of hostile workplace, threats of violence, hostile communications, etc. not reported to security or threat assessment team							
Employee/vendor terminations involving threats of violence							
No. personnel (HR, security, legal, other) trained in WPV response							

Information Risk Management[1]					
Percentage of key organizational functions for which a comprehensive strategy has been implemented					
Percentage of key external requirements for which the organization has been deemed by objective audit or other means to be in compliance					
Percentage of Information Security Program Principles for which approved policies and controls have been implemented by management					
Percentage of key information security management roles for which responsibilities, accountabilities, and authority are assigned and required skills identified					
Percentage of board meetings and/or designated committee meetings for which information security is on the agenda					
Percentage of security incidents that did not cause damage, compromise, or loss beyond established thresholds to the organization's assets, functions, or stakeholders					
Estimated damage or loss in dollars resulting from all security incidents					
Percentage of strategic partner and other third-party relationships for which information security requirements have been implemented in the agreements with these parties					
Percentage of organizational units with an established business continuity plan					
Percentage of required internal and external audits completed and reviewed by the Board					

Continued

Key Performance and Risk Indicators	Cost Management	Risk Management	ROI, Value	Legal Requirement	Policy Requirement	Life Safety	Internal Influence
Information Risk Management							
Percentage of audit findings that have been resolved							
Percentage of Information Security Program Elements for which approved policies and controls are currently operational							
Percentage of staff assigned responsibilities for information security policies and controls who have acknowledged accountability for their responsibilities in connection with those policies and controls							
Percentage of information security policy compliance reviews with no violations noted							
Percentage of business unit heads and senior managers who have implemented operational procedures to ensure compliance with approved information security policies and controls							
Percentage of new employees hired in this reporting period who satisfactorily completed security awareness training before being granted network access							
Percentage of employees who have satisfactorily completed periodic security awareness refresher training as required by policy							
Percentage of position descriptions that define the information security roles, responsibilities, skills, and certifications for: Security managers and administrators, IT personnel, and general staff system users							

Percentage of job performance reviews that include evaluation of information security responsibilities and information security policy compliance					
Percentage of user roles, systems, and applications that comply with the separation of duties principle					
Percentage of individuals with access to security software who are trained and authorized security administrators					
Percentage of individuals who are able to assign security privileges for systems and applications who are trained and authorized security administrators					
Percentage of individuals whose access privileges have been reviewed this reporting period: (1) employees with high level system and application privileges, (2) terminated employees, and (3) percentage of users who have undergone background checks					
Percentage of critical information assets and information-dependent functions for which some form of risk assessment has been performed and documented as required by policy					
Percentage of critical assets and functions for which the cost of compromise (loss, damage, disclosure, disruption in access to) has been quantified					
Percentage of identified risks that have a defined risk mitigation plan against which status is reported in accordance with policy					

Continued

Key Performance and Risk Indicators	Cost Management	Risk Management	ROI, Value	Legal Requirement	Policy Requirement	Life Safety	Internal Influence
Information Risk Management							
Percentage of known information security risks that are related to third-party relationships							
Percentage of critical information assets or functions for which access by third-party personnel is not allowed							
Percentage of third-party personnel with current information access privileges who have been reviewed by designated authority to have continued need for access in accordance with policy							
Percentage of systems with critical information assets or functions for which electronic connection by third-party systems is not allowed							
Percentage of security incidents that involved third-party personnel							
Percentage of third-party agreements that include/demonstrate external verification of policies and procedures							
Percentage of third-party relationships that have been reviewed for compliance with information security requirements							
Percentage of out-of-compliance review findings that have been corrected since the last review							
Percentage of information assets that have been reviewed and classified by the designated owner in accordance with the classification scheme established by policy							

Percentage of information assets with defined access privileges that have been assigned based on role and in accordance with policy					
Percentage of scheduled asset inventories that occurred on time according to policy					
Percentage of organizational units with a documented business continuity plan for which specific responsibilities have been assigned					
Percentage of business continuity plans that have been reviewed, exercised/tested, and updated in accordance with policy					
Percentage of information security risks related to systems architecture identified in the most recent risk assessment that have been adequately mitigated					
Percentage of system architecture changes (additions, modifications, or deletions) that were reviewed for security impacts, approved by appropriate authority, and documented via change request forms					
Percentage of critical information assets or functions residing on systems that are currently in compliance with the approved systems architecture					
Percentage of critical organizational information assets and functions that have been reviewed from the perspective of physical risks such as controlling physical access and physical protection of backup media					
Percentage of critical organizational information assets and functions exposed to physical risks for which risk mitigation actions have been implemented					

Continued

Key Performance and Risk Indicators	Cost Management	Risk Management	ROI, Value	Legal Requirement	Policy Requirement	Life Safety	Internal Influence
Information Risk Management							
Percentage of critical assets that have been reviewed from the perspective of environmental risks such as temperature, fire, flooding, etc.							
Percentage of servers in locations with controlled physical access							
Percentage of information security requirements from applicable laws and regulations that are included in the internal/external audit program and schedule							
Percentage of information security audits conducted in compliance with the approved internal/external audit program and schedule							
Percentage of management actions in response to audit findings/recommendations that were implemented as agreed as to timeliness and completeness							
No. active user IDs assigned to only one person							
Percentage of systems and applications that perform password policy verification							
Percentage of active user passwords that are set to expire in accordance with policy							
Percentage of systems with critical information assets that use stronger authentication than IDs and passwords in accordance with policy							
Percentage of systems where vendor-supplied accounts and passwords have been disabled or reset							

Percentage of computer user accounts assigned to personnel who have left the organization or no longer have need for access that have been closed				
Percentage of systems with account lockout parameters set in accordance with policy				
Percentage of inactive user accounts that have been disabled in accordance with policy				
Percentage of workstations with session time-out/automatic logout controls set in accordance with policy				
Percentage of active computer accounts that have been reviewed for justification of current access privileges in accordance with policy				
Percentage of systems where permission to install nonstandard software is limited in accordance with policy				
Percentage of systems and applications where assignment of user privileges is in compliance with the policy that specifies role-based information access privileges				
Percentage of systems for which approved configuration settings have been implemented as required by policy				
Percentage of systems with configurations that do not deviate from approved standards				
Percentage of systems that are continuously monitored for configuration policy compliance with out-of-compliance alarms or reports				
Percentage of systems whose configuration is compared with a previously established trusted baseline in accordance with policy				

Continued

Key Performance and Risk Indicators	Cost Management	Risk Management	ROI, Value	Legal Requirement	Policy Requirement	Life Safety	Internal Influence
Information Risk Management							
Percentage of systems where the authority to make configuration changes is limited in accordance with policy							
Percentage of systems for which event and activity logging has been implemented in accordance with policy							
Percentage of systems for which event and activity logs are monitored and reviewed in accordance with policy							
Percentage of systems for which log size and retention duration have been implemented in accordance with policy							
Percentage of systems that generate warnings about anomalous or potentially unauthorized activity							
Percentage of notebooks and mobile devices that are required to verify compliance with approved configuration policy prior to being granted network access							
Percentage of communication channels controlled by the organization that have been secured in accordance with policy							
Percentage of mobile users who access enterprise facilities using secure communications methods							
Percentage of workstations (including notebooks) with automatic protection in accordance with policy							
Percentage of servers with automatic protection in accordance with policy							

Percentage of mobile devices with automatic protection in accordance with policy				
Percentage of systems with the latest approved patches installed				
Mean time from vendor patch availability to patch installation by type of technology environment				
Percentage of software changes that were reviewed for security impacts in advance of installation				
Percentage of workstation firewalls, host firewalls, subnetwork firewalls, and perimeter firewalls configured in accordance with policy				
Percentage of critical information assets stored on network accessible devices that are encrypted with widely tested and published cryptographic algorithms				
Percentage of mobile computing devices using encryption for critical information assets in accordance with policy				
Percentage of passwords and pins that are encrypted (cryptographically one-way hashed) in accordance with policy				
Percentage of systems with critical information assets or functions that have been backed up in accordance with policy				
Percentage of systems with critical information assets or functions where restoration from a stored backup has been successfully demonstrated				
Percentage of backup media stored off-site in secure storage				

Continued

Key Performance and Risk Indicators	Cost Management	Risk Management	ROI, Value	Legal Requirement	Policy Requirement	Life Safety	Internal Influence
Information Risk Management							
Percentage of used backup media sanitized prior to reuse or disposal							
Percentage of operational time that critical services were unavailable (as seen by users and customers) due to security incidents							
Percentage of security incidents that exploited existing vulnerabilities with known solutions, patches, or workarounds							
Percentage of systems affected by security incidents that exploited existing vulnerabilities with known solutions, patches, or workarounds							
Percentage of security incidents that were managed in accordance with established policies, procedures, and processes							
Percentage of systems with critical information assets or functions that have been assessed for vulnerabilities in accordance with policy							
Percentage of vulnerability assessment findings that have been addressed since the last reporting period							
Business Continuity and Contingency Planning							
After-action reports indicate business function resumption occurred within defined timelines							
No. incidents where recovery was within the recovery time objective							
Incident impact (how much of whatever asset you are willing to lose) to the recovery point objective							

No. critical business functions by (high to lowest) uptime criticality sector			
No. most critical uptime business functions with tested/confirmed contingency plans			
No. critical functions with SPOFs			
No. or percentage of SPOFs with no alternate site (decreases or increases)			
The severity of action items resulting from test decreases			
No. and percentage of business units with up-to-date (or outdated) response plans			
By criticality of business functions			
No. or percentage of plans tested (walk through, actual, table top, call test, others)			
No. or percentage of critical business functions tested at alternate sites			
Incidents addressed with positive results that could have had major impact to critical business functions			
No. critical business functions' alternate seats by location			
Seats required vs available and ready			
Outage causes by location			
No. natural events resulting in business interruption by time			
Estimated frequency of similar events in the future (insurance data?)			
Critical business process downtime (in minutes per reporting period or event)			
Recovery time (to recover lost process, restore functionality, etc.)			

Continued

Key Performance and Risk Indicators	Cost Management	Risk Management	ROI, Value	Legal Requirement	Policy Requirement	Life Safety	Internal Influence
Information Risk Management							
Percentage of business units owning highly critical business processes demonstrates fully competent business continuity planners							
Business-Based Security Programs							
No. unappointed and untrained personnel within the decentralized information security functions							
No. unappointed and untrained personnel within the decentralized business continuity/contingency planning functions							
No. unappointed and untrained personnel within the decentralized business-related (fraud prevention or investigation, or other) security functions							
Percentage of appointed and trained vs unappointed and untrained personnel within the decentralized security functions of selected business units							
Business ventures (foreign travel, offshore software development, acquisitions) without conscious recognition or understanding of potential security vulnerabilities							
Percentage of leased property with adequate (or inadequate) security							
No. internal incidents where failures in manager/supervisory oversight is cited as a causal factor							

Metric					
No. incidents by location, type, and building where security policy was not followed or absence of security awareness was contributory to the incident					
No. incidents in which business units failed to report or involve corporate security					
Knowledge of domestic restraining order, unreported prior WPV, or other risky conditions with resulting risk exposure					
Percentage of turnover for key security positions by location and/or type					
Incidents attributable to absence of knowledge of security policy by individuals involved					
Supply Management Security Objectives					
Management, Professional Development, and Employee Satisfaction					
Turnover rates (particularly for contract security service providers)					
Percentage of positions filled from within vs external recruitment					
Cost of employee selection (exempt and nonexempt)					
Cost of recruitment and selection by location					
Turnover by location					
Ratio of employees with security-related certifications earned by examination per total security					
Ratio of general security certifications to total security population					
No. emergency medical technicians (EMT) or other first responder credentials per served population					

Continued

—cont'd

Key Performance and Risk Indicators	Cost Management	Risk Management	ROI, Value	Legal Requirement	Policy Requirement	Life Safety	Internal Influence
Management, Professional Development, and Employee Satisfaction							
Ratio of investigative certifications to total security population							
Ratio of information security certifications to total security population (or IT population)							
Ratio of business continuity professional certifications to total security population (or population within highest criticality business processes)							
No. hours compensated for professional development							
Annual budget variance (for department, by organizational unit, by cost center manager, etc.)							
Volume of personnel-related complaints and administrative actions (by organizational unit, location, employee category, etc.)							
Metrics Program Objectives							
Measurable indicators that our metrics are positively influencing corporate action, attitudes, and policy							
Measurable indicators that our metrics are materially impacting exposure to loss							
Measurable indicators that our metrics demonstrate security's alignment with the business strategy and objectives							
Measurable indicators that our metrics are enabling proactive management of the corporate security program							

Measure					
Measurable indicators that our metrics accurately reflect levels of success or failure of security programs					
Measurable indicators that competitors or industry benchmarks are collaboratively utilizing metrics to demonstrate [designated] ROI					
Contract Guard Force Performance Measures					
Percentage rejected by preassignment standard per site per quarter					
No. assigned and dismissed within 90 days per site per quarter					
Percentage assigned appropriately certified by state requirements where applicable					
Percentage assigned who indicate lack of knowledge of security procedures					
Percentage assigned from reserve pool failing to meet preassignment requirements					
Percentage assigned failing to meet language and writing proficiency					
All assigned officers possess basic word processing competency for report preparation					
All assigned officers have a clean driving record					
No. shifts per site per period with officers working in excess of 12 h					
Percentage of candidates rejected for assignment per site per quarter					
Vendor has an established performance appraisal process consistent with required competencies					

Continued

Key Performance and Risk Indicators	Cost Management	Risk Management	ROI, Value	Legal Requirement	Policy Requirement	Life Safety	Internal Influence
Contract Guard Force Performance Measures							
100% of owner items or equipment assigned to vendor at each location is accounted for							
Percentage of incidents where supervisory interaction with officer was sought or provided to improve knowledge and/or quality of response							
Percentage assigned with in excess of [specify percentage] deficient incident reports per period							
Absentee rates per site requiring assignment from reserve pool							
Guard tour equipment is operational at each site scheduled for deployment							
Percentage of guard tours completed as programmed per shift and reporting period							
Percentage of missed guard tours with no documentation							
Logs, communications, and dispatch quality indicate console operators are knowledgeable and customer-focused							
Logs indicate response times to incidents and calls for service consistent with urgency of risk							
Percentage of incident reports containing essential data for resolution and/or follow-up							
Percentage of incident reports with supervisory sign-off per period							
No. hazards found by inspections, tours, or officer initiative per site per period							

Percentage of found hazards resolved per site per period					
Percentage of compliments/complaints per officer per quarter					
Post orders at all sites are up-to-date, anno-tated, and all officers have been made aware of operational changes					
100% Site compliance—Local lead supervisor has developed and updates a site security plan keyed to local threats, risks, and business safety and security requirements					
100% Site compliance—When nonroutine events occur, local lead supervisor provides timely and accurate reports to designated owner representatives and takes remedial action(s) as directed					
100% of investigations conducted by vendor staff are consistent with procedures estab-lished by corporate security representatives					
Percentage of pass/fail drug testing per site per quarter					
Percentage of pass/fail random drug testing per site per quarter					
Percentage of incident reports received and approved on time per reporting period					
Spot inspections indicate lists are maintained for personnel in buildings during nonbusiness hours for each building					
Test procedure utilized to confirm retention of training materials					

Continued

Key Performance and Risk Indicators	Cost Management	Risk Management	ROI, Value	Legal Requirement	Policy Requirement	Life Safety	Internal Influence
Contract Guard Force Performance Measures							
100% Site compliance—Procedures are in place to protect confidential information or information required to be protected in accordance with regulation(s)							
100% of alarm devices/points and controlled access portals are tested on schedule and repairs made as required							
100% of temporary access badges issued were visitor acknowledged, returned, or appropriately dated for expiration							
100% Site compliance—Procedures for screening authorized vs unauthorized personnel and property are in place and effective							
Monthly emergency response testing to include at least one of the following: duress alarm activations, medical emergency response, fire alarm, threatening phone calls, and vital equipment alarms. Analysis takes into account objectives and results with summary of corrective actions							
Procedures are in place and effective for ensuring effective communication of information between shifts							
Daily postinspections per shift indicate status of post and resolution of any noted deficiencies							
Administer key/core system and records as appropriate to site requirements							
100% of response time objectives met per period for events requiring a posted duration							

100% assigned officers have completed 36h of preassignment training			
Required customer service and hospitality/concierge training			
Periodic refresher training is delivered and documented in officer files			
100% of officers are up-to-date and certified in CPR/AED, first aid, blood-borne pathogens, hazardous materials, and state mandated training as required			
100% of all supervisors assigned to site(s) are trained in accordance with requirements			
Vendor provides a training coordinator and trainers with requisite specializations as required			
100% of assigned security personnel demonstrate familiarity with procedures associated with demonstrations, building evacuations, potential business outage, or other contingency events			
100% of invoices are entered within 5 business days of receipt and verifiably correct			
Vendor provides an off-site supervisor on a quarterly basis to review site security operations and document and addresses all deficiencies			
Monthly supervisory review to include evaluation of response to alarm dispatches and results. Analysis takes into account the no. alarms received, the no. times security personnel were dispatched, and quantity and quality of completed incident reports			

Continued

Key Performance and Risk Indicators	Cost Management	Risk Management	ROI, Value	Legal Requirement	Policy Requirement	Life Safety	Internal Influence
Security Command and Control Center Measures							
Maintain or improve response time to call for service							
Manage call queue for nonservice/info only calls							
Provide for the required complement of qualified and trained operators							
Provide for workload surge backup							
Maintain dispatch time to goal							
Maintain all logs, incident documentation, and equipment malfunction tickets							
Maintain levels of call-taking accuracy to goal							
Measure, maintain, and report on vendor service level agreements (if applicable)							
Increase call intake and dispatch process while not increasing time to dispatch							
Maintain customer confidence in responsiveness to calls for service							
Maintain uptime reliability of critical monitoring and dispatch equipment at 99.90%							
Maintain staff turnover to goal							
Provide improved support to officers safety and customer service							
Improve timely and accurate completion of incident reporting							
Provide timely and responsive support to business units during escalated event management							
Provide productive and efficient operational environment							
Ensure levels of operator knowledge for all assigned Boeing facilities							

Metric				
Provide for contingency event relocation on a preestablished response time				
Test all primary and backup equipment on a scheduled basis				
Reduce rates of false and nuisance alarms				
Provide for and maintain shift hand-off procedures				
Maintain mean time between failures of critical security operations center (SOC) equipment at goal				
Maintain mean time to repair for critical SOC equipment at goal				
Monitor and report on targeted response times for emergency calls for service				
Percentage Dispatch Time @ Goal				
Call-Taking Accuracy (sampled percentage)				
System Availability and Accessibility				
Vendor service level agreement (SLA) compliance percentage to goal				
Failover Test Result				
Operations Audit Result				
Call Service Level Compliance				
First Call Resolution Rate				
Staff Retention Rate				
Call Transfer Rate				

BI, background investigation; WPV, workplace violence; SPOF, single point of failure.
'On November 17, 2004, the Corporate Information Security Working Group of the United States House of Representatives issued its "Report of Best Practices and Metrics Teams" suggested for boards of directors' use in connection with its information security responsibilities. Because the information in this report is so comprehensive and ideally keyed to the purpose of this publication, the core metrics identified in Section VIII of the report are reproduced here. The complete report is available online (https://net.educause.edu/ir/library/pdf/CSD3661.pdf, last revised January 10, 2005) and contains a wealth of advice on the use of metrics in general and for information security in particular.

Appendix 2 Sample High-Level Security Work Breakdown Structure

Security Program Element	Cost	Measures and Metrics		
1. Program Administration				
1.1 Budget and finance				
1.2 Planning and program development				
1.3 Policy and standards				
1.4 Personnel management				
1.4.1 Performance measurement				
1.4.2 Personnel development				
1.4.2.1 Core competency analysis				
1.4.3 Job analysis and recruiting				
1.4.4 Skills training				
1.4.5 Time tracking				
1.5 Data analysis and reporting				
1.5.1 Lessons-learned analysis				
1.5.2 Management reporting				
1.5.3 Trend analysis				
1.5.4 Specific crime analysis				
1.5.5 Procurement activities				
1.6 Inspection and review				
1.7 Contract management				
2. Technology Management				
2.1 Research and development				
2.2 System design guidelines				
2.3 Project management				
2.4 Equipment procurement				
2.4.1 Inventory management				
2.5 System design and engineering				
2.6 System installation				
2.6.1 System maintenance				
2.7 Fire/and life/safety systems				

Continued

—cont'd

Security Program Element	Cost	Measures and Metrics		
3. Access Administration				
3.1 Logical access administration				
3.2 Physical access administration				
3.2.1 Badging and orientation				
4. Risk Management				
4.1 SPOF analysis				
4.2 Alarm abatement				
4.3 Vulnerability analysis				
4.4 Risk/cost analysis				
4.5 Risk reporting				
4.6 Risk mitigation activities				
4.6.1 Fraud prevention				
4.6.2 Proactive patrol				
4.6.3 Hazard identification				
4.6.4 Life/safety program				
4.6.5 Alarm monitoring				
4.6.6 Central dispatching				
4.6.7 Emergency management				
4.6.8 Computer virus response				
4.6.9 Information security (INFOSEC) response (computer security event response team (CSERT))				
4.6.10 Executive protection program				
5. Investigation				
5.1 Background investigation				
5.2 Due diligence examination				
5.3 Criminal investigation				
5.4 Incident response				
5.4.1 Incident reporting				
5.5 Specialized/directed reporting				
5.6 Case management				
5.6.1 File management				
5.7 Law enforcement liaison				
5.8 Workplace violence threat assessment				
5.9 Information security compromise				

Security Program Element	Cost	Measures and Metrics		
6. Risk Communication and Business Unit Skills				
6.1 Governance unit liaison				
6.2 Employee orientation–security				
6.3 Cross-security communication				
6.4 Communication with business units				
6.5 Security committee liaison				
6.6 Information security skills development				
6.7 Development of awareness material				
6.7.1 Security awareness program				
6.8 Fraud prevention training				
6.9 Floor warden training				
6.10 Business continuity planner training and awareness				
7. Business Continuity Planning				
7.1 Emergency notification listing				
7.2 Plan development and maintenance				
7.3 Plan review and administration				
7.4 Business function criticality lists				
7.5 Plan testing				
7.6 Alternate site support/critical spares support				
7.7 Testing and maintenance				
8. Information Security Administration				
8.1 Information security consulting				
8.2 Information security engineering				
8.3 Proprietary InfoSecurity program administration				
8.4 Information security risk assessment				
8.5 Compliance monitoring				
8.5.1 Systems/safeguards audit				
8.6 Safeguards installation/maintain				
8.7 Chief information officer (CIO)/IT liaison				

Appendix 3   Risk Measure Maps

Frequency and severity of workplace violence incidents

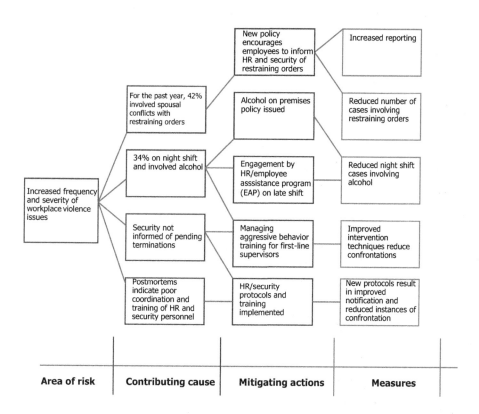

Area of risk	Contributing cause	Mitigating actions	Measures

Increased numbers of employees as subjects in misconduct cases

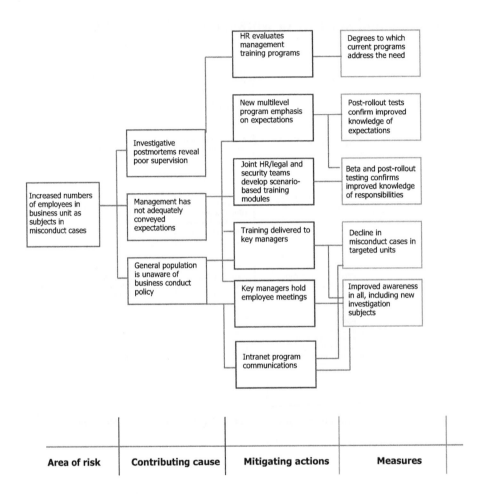

| Area of risk | Contributing cause | Mitigating actions | Measures |

Business interruption by computer virus

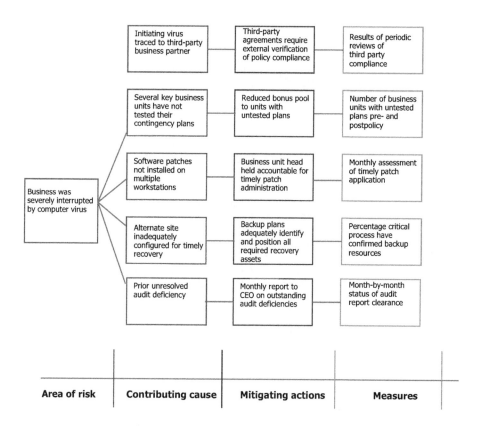

| Area of risk | Contributing cause | Mitigating actions | Measures |

Security budget reduction as a result of decreasing corporate revenues

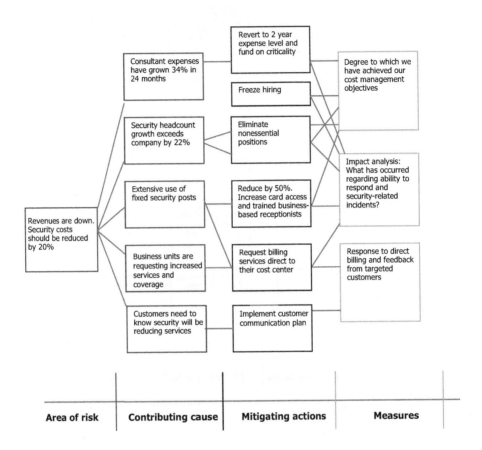

Failure of security to respond to security breach

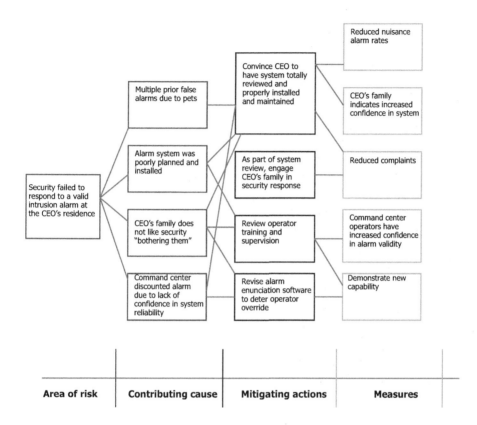

| Area of risk | Contributing cause | Mitigating actions | Measures |

About Elsevier's Security Executive Council Risk Management Portfolio

Elsevier's Security Executive Council Risk Management Portfolio is the voice of the security leader. It equips executives, practitioners, and educators with research-based, proven information and practical solutions for successful security and risk management programs. This portfolio covers topics in the areas of risk mitigation and assessment, ideation and implementation, and professional development. It brings trusted operational research, risk management advice, tactics, and tools to business professionals. Previously available only to the Security Executive Council community, this content—covering corporate security, enterprise crisis management, global IT security, and more—provides real-world solutions and "how-to" applications. This portfolio enables business and security executives, security practitioners, and educators to implement new physical and digital risk management strategies and build successful security and risk management programs.

Elsevier's Security Executive Council Risk Management Portfolio is a key part of the **Elsevier Risk Management & Security Collection**. The collection provides a complete portfolio of titles for the business executive, practitioner, and educator by bringing together the best imprints in risk management, security leadership, digital forensics, IT security, physical security, homeland security, and emergency management: Syngress that provides cutting-edge computer and information security material; Butterworth–Heinemann, the premier security, risk management, homeland security, and disaster-preparedness publisher; and Anderson Publishing, a leader in criminal justice publishing for more than 40 years. These imprints, along with the addition of Security Executive Council content, bring the work of highly regarded authors into one prestigious, complete collection.

The Security Executive Council (www.securityexecutivecouncil.com) is a leading problem-solving research and services organization focused on helping businesses build value while improving their ability to effectively manage and mitigate risk. Drawing on the collective knowledge of a large community of successful security practitioners, experts, and strategic alliance partners, the Council develops strategy and insight and identifies proven practices that cannot be found anywhere else. Their research, services, and tools are focused on protecting people, brand, information, physical assets, and the bottom line.

Elsevier (www.elsevier.com) is an international multimedia publishing company that provides world-class information and innovative solutions tools. It is part of Reed Elsevier, a world-leading provider of professional information solutions in the science, medical, risk, legal, and business sectors.

Index

Printed and bound by CPI Group (UK) Ltd, Croydon, CR0 4YY

08/05/2025

01864909-0003